Reference

BLACK PEOPLE IN THE METHODIST CHURCH
Whither Thou Goest?

William B. McClain

ABINGDON PRESS

Nashville

BLACK PEOPLE IN THE METHODIST CHURCH
WHITHER THOU GOEST?

Copyright © 1984 by William B. McClain

This book is printed on acid-free paper.

Library of Congress Cataloging-in-Publication Data

McClain, William B.
  Black people in the Methodist Church : whither thou goest? / William B. McClain.
    p. cm.
  Reprint. Originally published: Cambridge, Mass. : Schenkman, © 1984.
  Includes bibliographical references and index.
  ISBN 0-687-03588-0 (alk. paper)
  1. Afro-American Methodists—History. 2. Methodist Church—United States—History. 3. United Methodist Church (U.S.)—History. I. Title.
BX8435.M37 1990
287′.6′08996073—dc20   90-39377
                                                                 CIP

Formerly published under ISBN 0-87073-724-4 and 0-87073-770-8 by Schenkman Publishing Co., Inc., 190 Concord Ave., Cambridge MA 02138.

96 97 98 99 00 01 02 03 04 — 10 9 8 7 6 5 4 3

MANUFACTURED IN THE UNITED STATES OF AMERICA

TABLE OF CONTENTS

ACKNOWLEDGEMENTS

I wish to acknowledge my gratitude to Dr. C. Eric Lincoln who read the original manuscript and offered valuable criticisms and suggestions. Perhaps much more than that, he provided the inspiration and reason for writing this book in the first place. My teacher, mentor, confidante and long-time friend, I am eternally grateful to him. He is one of the two persons to whom this book is dedicated.

The following people read the manuscript, offered help or provided means to enable the completion and publication of this book: Ms. Peggy Billings, Dr. Gilbert H. Caldwell, Rev. John W. Coleman, Ms. Virginia Hamner, Mr. Louis Hodge, Dr. James C. Logan, Dr. C. Leonard Miller, Dr. Tex S. Sample, Ms. Edith Spurr, and Dr. Woodie White.

A word of personal gratitude is offered to Bishop James S. Thomas of the East Ohio Area. Not only did he consent to write the Foreword for this book after reading the original manuscript, but throughout my continuing journey in the ministry, he has been a model and has offered sound advice when sometimes it seemed futile to keep on going. I owe him more than I have ever told him—knowing him, it would probably embarrass him. His faithful contribution to the church in the midst of confusing times has been largely understated and probably unrecognized. He is rare among God's creations. Always gentle and tough about the things that matter most, he has helped many of us to stay when leaving seemed so much easier.

A special thanks to my editor, Mrs. Deborah Rampino Gorman, who offered valuable help, suggestions and counsel. Her careful editorial assistance improved considerably an original draft. In this work, as in every other endeavor, Deborah approached it with *tough* care; she continues as a faithful friend. I also owe a debt of thanks to Ms. Paula Budin and Ms. Dian Hunter of Wesley Theological Seminary for their invaluable secretarial assistance.

There are others, like several members of St. Paul United Methodist Church, Oxon Hill, Maryland and other black Methodists who insisted that I go ahead and complete this publication. To all of them I owe a great deal of thanks.

As always, and in everything, my wife, Jo Ann, offered support, encouragement and help. She typed the original manuscript and labored alongside me to see that this book reached the publisher. She alone knows all the agonies experienced to get this book in print. Without her this publication would not be. My gratitude to her is far greater than my ability to express it.

I am grateful to all of those listed and acknowledged and many others unnamed, but hold none of them responsible for what is written and contained within these pages. They improved upon what was originally written, but I accept full responsibility for the final version of this book.

A WORD OF DEDICATION AND GRATITUDE

This book is dedicated to two black United Methodist ministers: the Rev. Lindsay Garfield Fields, and the Rev. C. Eric Lincoln.

Lindsay Garfield Fields, now retired after more than fifty (50) years in the active ministry of the several versions of Methodism, inspired me to find my way into the Methodist ministry, and has always been more than pastor to me—but also father, provider, friend, model and confidante. He has moved across the black church and the whole church without much notice or noise—but those who have encountered him, as he has kept his charge, are unforgettably aware that he is a servant of the Lord always on an important errand. He is truly a steward of a mystery who has followed faithfully this church throughout its changes and will serve it until he dies.

C. Eric Lincoln, my major professor at Clark College, Atlanta, Georgia, and now professor of Religion and Culture at Duke University, took what L. G. Fields had taught and inspired in me and shaped and molded that into critical scholarship and faithful commitment to the black church. My debt to him is greater than can be paid in these pages or anywhere else.

Both of these men have insisted on excellence in themselves and others, and given so much to many—most of the time without ever mentioning what they gave. The dedication of this book to them is simply an effort on the part of one who has received so much from each of them to express, in a small way, a large measure of gratitude owed to them by many like me.

The title of this work grows out of a reflection on their lives and commitment as much as it attempts to capture the spirit and story of black people who are Methodist, who have remained Methodist and followed wherever the Church has gone. I cannot help but add: they have both longed to see the majority church and "a church within a church," become *one* pluralistic church—the church of Jesus Christ, where divisiveness loses its significance and differences are accepted and applauded, and the Christ becomes Lord of all. I learned to have that hope from them. I reaffirm it now.

FOREWORD

It has been almost forty years since Gunnar Myrdal wrote about our American dilemma. Looking back now, it is difficult to see why this book caused some Americans so much surprise. The dilemma, wrote Myrdal, was that this nation, so deeply committed to the freedom of all people, had yet to rise above deep divisions based on race, the rigid segregation enforced by law, and the powerful institutions of silent—but no less lethal—discrimination which saw a widening gap between the fortunes of the black and white races. That this should have been a surprise to anyone is itself a dilemma. For it is one thing to present documentable forms of institutional discrimination—any sociologist could analyze these without looking very hard—but it is quite another thing, an even more serious offense, to become so accustomed to such systems that it somehow seems right.

Much has happened in American society since 1944. More has happened in the surrounding world of nations. The discovery and use of atomic power, the rise of liberation movements world-wide, the founding of new and self-governing nations in Africa, the unusual swift movement of peoples across the world—all of these suddenly make a world community where no nation is very far from any other. Added to or within these massive social movements, we experienced the legal assaults upon structural segregation, the Civil Rights movement of the 1950s and 60s, the rise of black power, the passage of the Civil Rights bills, the massive voter registration of blacks, and now the experience of the new dilemma—being in and out at the same time. Therefore, what Myrdal set forth as the dilemma of 1944 is an even more complex dilemma of 1984. If being legally out is painful, in a nation whose documents literally shout inclusion, it is hardly less painful to be in and out of fellowship in a church where inclusiveness should not be debatable at all.

While this may seem to be far afield for a writer on the black presence in the United Methodist Church, it is, in fact, the only context in which the black church can be properly understood. And this is for at least two primary reasons.

First, the United Methodist Church, and all its predecessors, grew up with and mirrored this nation in their dominant attitudes toward the black presence. All major denominations were divided over the issue of slavery. While the very young Methodist Church took a very strong stand against slavery, it was a position that could not be maintained under the pressures of social reality. When, after some time, the Church had to face up to the problem of race, it did so by separate black Annual Conferences, dating back to the end of legal slavery. Long decades passed before the major bodies of Methodism were united again. And again the question arose: "What, now, of the black presence?" The answer this time was structural segregation, the Central Jurisdiction, which existed from 1940 to 1967. Therefore, both as great contributor to and mirror of the culture, the Methodist Church had—and has—its own dilemma.

Second, at the heart of this dilemma, both for church and nation, is what might be called the great anomaly. By all New Testament standards accepted by major denominations, it is the rule to be inclusive. But that is so much easier said than done. These are more stable interracial churches now than there were in 1944 when Howard Thurman started one in San Francisco. These are the exceptions, however, and not the rule. For many and complex reasons, the rule in this country is separate local churches for black and white. And if one says that the major reason for this is residential segregation, one still has to explain why thousands of church members, black and white, drive by some churches to attend the one of their preference.

This anomaly is seen again in higher education, in employment, and in legal precedents. Consider how righteous is the cry against "reverse discrimination" when a few uncertain moves have been made to correct the massive discrimination of three and a half centuries. To some people, it is a cause for alarm when there are one or two attempts to break into systems which cannot stand the scrutiny of this nation's creed. They stand over against the ideal of national commitment, but this hardly affects their practice. Or, consider, the righteous intent to integrate all black colleges, which from their founding were open to all people, by declaring that white colleges with only twenty years of carefully measured integration have suddenly become the rule. Which is rule; which anomaly?

All of this is strange, even revolutionary, to those who find the progress of the last twenty years so great as to leave no further major problems of race. If that can be said by a president of the United States in 1981, it certainly can be believed by many others now. Myrdal's dilemma, then, is still with us but not as easily identified. The complexity and subtlety of the issues now make it difficult even to state the case as sharply as it ought to be stated.

For the reasons stated above, this book is of great importance to all who would understand better the Church's need to be moving toward full inclusiveness. Himself a product of the old Central Jurisdiction, Dr. McClain has provided both the historical understanding of the issues and the prophetic question. An able participant in the several "worlds" of race, he has looked at the problems about which he writes both with the scholar's critical vision and the preacher's passion to have things appear as they actually are and to be what Christ would have them be.

Nor is this book among the hopeless journeys into the netherworld where dilemma simply compounds dilemma. There are no easy answers. But there is the picture of vigor shown in those black leaders who, with much less opportunity to live and work in the wider church, left a rich heritage for younger black leaders to emulate and extend.

"Whither thou goest?" is an appropriate question for any

church at any time. To raise such a question at all is to imply an answer of some sort. Whether that answer will come by pious withdrawal from cultural pressures into an individualistic kind of religion or by a clear understanding of history and prophetic action is largely left to the leadership of the Church. But I do not speak here of supervising leadership alone; that can only go so far. I speak also of the writer, the scholar, the preacher who is empowered by a great urge to know and share the truth that will make all of us free.

James S. Thomas
Bishop
East Ohio Conference
United Methodist Church

I
INTRODUCTION:
A Checkered History

The Wesleyan tradition, to which the present United Methodist Church is heir, began with an evangelical zeal directed toward the lower classes, the poor and the dispossessed. Although its founder, John Wesley, and his brother Charles, the poet of Methodism, could hardly be classified as lower class, the Methodist movement which they started was rooted in a passionate and enthusiastic concern for the poorer classes. Wesley preached a gospel of salvation to the miners and day laborers, to those who worked in the factories at Bristol and inhabited the gloomy and dingy slums of London, and other large cities of England. He, himself, was a graduate of Oxford and bore its *ineffaceable* stamp. He attracted to the Methodist movement as its initial leaders those of similar background and learning: George Whitefield, a graduate of Pembroke College, Oxford, acclaimed as one of the most powerful preachers of all times, joined the Wesleys and became one of the Oxford Methodists. Dr. Thomas Coke, a university man like the Wesleys and Whitefield, and a Welshman of considerable means, became Wesley's chosen spokesman and crossed the Atlantic no fewer than eighteen times at his own expense to give leadership to the fledgling Methodist movement. And then there was Francis Asbury, who accompanied Coke. Although he was not a university graduate, like Wesley he was well-read and believed in education. He is reported to have

1

had a fixed rule to read one hundred pages daily, mastering Greek, Latin and Hebrew.

These middle-class leaders established a church of the poor in England that later blossomed in the latter part of the eighteenth century on the frontiers of America. These soul-hunting circuit riders rode across this land, finding lodging in the rough cabins of the pioneers and making tracks through virtually untrodden forests and into the urban areas along the Atlantic seacoast, to proclaim a simple gospel of salvation to all who would listen.

The poor and the disinherited, the unchurched and the uneducated listened gladly to the call to repentance under the threat of damnation. The Methodist preachers told of a Christ that Wesley had discovered at Aldersgate who offers an inner assurance of love causing the heart to feel strangely warmed. This simple message was good news to the hard-working, God-fearing, common people who populated the perimeter of colonial America, and they responded with en-thusiastic emotionalism to the Methodist evangelical vision of Christianity. Group after group were brought into the church because of a loving acceptance which could prevail over the rejections found elsewhere.

It used to be said that the Episcopal priests waited for the trains with velvet-covered seats to go West, while the Pres-byterian clergy went in covered wagons with the migrants before the railroads were built. The Methodist preachers, by contrast, rode on horseback ahead of the people and greeted them as they arrived. Despite allowances for exaggeration by Methodists, there is some truth to that saying, as it appears in an emblem which features a circuit rider seated on a horse, reading a book associated with the United Methodist denomination.

By the time of the first annual conference in 1773, these itinerant preachers had penetrated the settled coastal regions and were keeping abreast of a population that was threading its way westward through the Appalachian barriers and along the rivers that led to isolated places. At that first annual conference, appointments of preachers were made for a region extending from New York City southward, to Norfolk and Petersburg in Virginia, and westward to Philadelphia. Joseph Pilmoor had volunteered to come from England to America, and had made a preaching excursion from Philadelphia to Savannah. Richard Boardman, his English comrade, had gone as far north as Boston to stake out the claim for Methodism in New England.

Among the poor and disinherited who listened and responded to the gospel message of the Methodist preachers were the black slaves who had been brought to America in chains. They joined the Methodist "classes" and "societies" and attended the preaching events and camp meetings. Perhaps, "For the slave," as Harry V. Richardson points out, "becoming a Christian represented a complex of aims and hopes in which his soul's salvation was only one."[1] In any case, the black diaspora from the West African motherland responded. There was immediate and rapid growth among the black Methodists. In some cases, the number of black people equalled or exceeded the white people. Thomas Rankin, a white Methodist preacher in Virginia, reports this response to his preaching in 1776:

> At four in the afternoon I preached again . . . I had gone through about two-thirds of my discourse, and was bringing the words home to the present *now*, when such power descended that hundreds fell to the ground, and the house seemed to shake with the presence of God. The chapel was full of white and black, and many were without that could not get in. Look wherever we would, we saw nothing but streaming eyes and faces bathed in tears; and heard nothing but groans and strong cries after God and the Lord Jesus Christ.
>
> Sunday 7. I preached at W's chapel, about twenty miles from Mr. J's. I intended to preach near the house, under the shade of some large trees. But the rain made it impracticable. The house was greatly crowded, and four or five hundred stood at the windows, and listened with unabated attention. I

[1] Harry V. Richardson, *Dark Salvation* (Garden City, N.Y.: Anchor Press, 1976), p. 47.

preached from Ezekiel's vision of dry bones: "And there was a great shaking." I was obliged to stop again and again, and beg of the people to compose themselves. But they could not; some on their knees, and some on their faces, were crying mightily to God all the time I was preaching. *Hundreds of Negroes* were among them, with tears streaming down their faces.[2]

Freeborn Garrettson, another of the Methodist itinerant preachers, describes the response of the slaves to his preaching in North Carolina:

In September I went to North Carolina, to travel Roanoak circuit, and was sweetly drawn out in to the glorious work, though my exercises were very great particularly respecting the slavery, and hard usage of the poor afflicted negroes. Many times did my heart ache on their account, and many tears ran down my cheeks, both in Virginia and Carolina, while exhibiting a crucified Jesus to their view; and I bless God that my labors were not in vain among them. I endeavored frequently to inculcate the doctrine of freedom in a private way, and this procured me the ill will of some, who were in that unmerciful practice. I would often set apart times to preach to the blacks, and adapt my discourse to them alone; and precious moments have I had. While many of their sable faces were bedewed with tears, their withered hands of faith were stretched out, and their precious souls made white in the blood of the Lamb. The suffering of those poor out-casts of men, through the blessing of God, drove them near to the Lord, and many of them were amazingly happy.[3]

It is the experiences of these black people who joined the Methodist movement from the very start, who found their spiritual home in the Methodist Episcopal Church, and who have remained a part of this body throughout its social metamorphosis, its changing structure, and its checkered history, that the following pages will recount and analyze. Present throughout this unfolding drama, beginning with

---

[2]Nathan Bangs, *A History of the Methodist Episcopal Church*, New York: Vol. I, pp. 111f., 1838.

[3]*The Experience and Travels of Mr. Freeborn Garretson* (Philadelphia: Parry Hall, 1791), pp. 76f.

the first organized Methodist Society at Sam's Creek in Frederick County, Maryland, and continuing through the last General Conference of the United Methodist Church, is the all-too-familiar question: What shall we do with the blacks? That question has a history of disillusioning and uncertain answers. The question black Methodists may have to answer for themselves is whether in the grand community of United Methodism they are a saving remnant or a sedimental (and perhaps sentimental) residue.

II

JOHN WESLEY ON SLAVERY:
Evangelist and Moralist

THE HOLY NAMELESS TWO

According to John Wesley's *Journal*, he baptized his first black converts on November 29, 1758, and received them into the Methodist movement. One of these two converts was a black woman. As he records it in his *Journal:*

> I rode to Wandsworth and baptized two Negroes belonging to Mr. Gilbert, a gentleman, lately from Antigua. One of these was deeply convinced of sin; the other is rejoicing in God her Savior and is the first African Christian I have known.[1]

These new converts, influenced by Wesley's preaching of an experiential faith through which persons are brought into a redeeming conscious fellowship with God, were so imbued with an evangelistic zeal that they went home and witnessed so persuasively to their experience that their owner, Nathaniel Gilbert, also became converted to the Christian faith. Gilbert was subsequently licensed as a local preacher in the Methodist movement.

When the three of them returned to the West Indies, they established the first Methodist chapel in the New World. That first meeting place was Gilbert's home. They obviously continued their persuasive witnessing, for by 1786, there were 1,569 members, only two of whom were white. J.

---

[1] *The Works of the Reverend John Wesley* (New York: J. Emory and B. Waugh, 1831), Vol. IV, p. 12.

Robinson Gregory, in reporting on the growth of Methodism in the West Indies, indicates that "the first Methodist Chapel in the Torrid Zone was set up in Antigua, composed almost wholly of Negroes."[2] Ten years later, Thomas Coke reports that the West Indian Missions had increased to more than 10,000 black members.[3] Unfortunately, neither Wesley nor Coke tells us who these "flaming" black evangels were who introduced Nathaniel Gilbert to Christ and thereby opened the way for Methodism to spread to the islands of the West Indies. We do not know who these first black Methodists were, but The Holy Nameless Two were certainly freed from the bondage of their sins, if not the bonds of their bodily existence. And let it not be said of them *Sic Transit Gloria Mundi:* Thus passes away the glory of their world.

Their memorial did not perish with them. Millions of blacks around the world have known the heart-warming assurance of God's love through Jesus Christ under the influence of the preaching successors of Wesley in the Methodist Church. And even those blacks who later found the racial and social conditions in the white Methodist Church intolerable at such places as St. George's Church in Philadelphia and John Street Methodist Episcopal Church in New York City, shared with The Holy Nameless Two and Wesley the bias for personalistic religion, evangelical theology, and the polity of Methodism.

The African Methodist Episcopal Church, founded by Richard Allen in 1796, and the African Methodist Episcopal Church Zion, separating out of the John Street Church a few years later, established themselves as *Methodist* Churches. They did not condemn the doctrines nor did they repudiate the polity of traditional Methodism. These were adopted by both African Methodist bodies with few changes and these black churches stand as bulwarks against racism. But the African Methodist Churches are also memorials to The Holy Nameless Two that Wesley baptized on that November day

[2] J. Robinson Gregory, *A History of Methodism* (London: Charles H. Kelley, 1911), Vol. I, p. 180.
[3] *Ibid.*, p. 220.

in 1758 in England. Their existence is still an indictment against the white church which professed the faith but practiced racism. Nor did the ever present question of being black and Methodist that they raised pass with them. In 1973, Gilbert Caldwell, a black United Methodist preacher and the son of a United Methodist preacher, was still raising the ultimate question behind the question: *Can Blacks Be Christian?*[4]

The Holy Nameless Two becoming Methodists first raised the question for Methodism about the relationship between evangelical Christianity and its prophetic roots. Would the Methodists transform a revolutionary ethic of Jesus, a humanitarianism born out of love, into an inoffensive prudential morality? What was to be the Methodists' stance on slavery? Was the Methodist movement to become a replica of the Church of England with its formalistic, cold religion and its class distinctions; its disdain for the poor, the disinherited, and disenfranchised; which a constellation of nonconforming founders of the Methodist movement had fought against? Where were the austere, scholarly fathers of "scriptural-holiness-spreading" Methodism to stand on the issue of human slavery?

WESLEY'S ANTISLAVERY STANCE

Wesley had been to America and had chanced to observe first hand the American form of slavery in operation. He came to the colony of Georgia upon the invitation of General James Oglethorpe in 1735. Both Oglethorpe and Wesley were attracted to Georgia because it was founded "to relieve the distressed." And, as William Phipps points out in an article in *Quarterly Review*, "because they presumed that slavery was a 'horrid crime' that would not be allowed in a colony devoted to Christian principles."[5]

---

[4]Gilbert H. Caldwell (Nashville: United Methodist Board of Discipleship, Graded Press, 1973). Dr. Caldwell's opening sentence is revealing: "The events of recent years cause us to ask, can blacks be Christian, can any young black person be Christian? p. 1.

[5]William Phipps, John Wesley on Slavery, *Quarterly Review*, Vol. 1, No. 1 (Summer, 1981).

The trustees of the Georgia Colony had placed a ban on slavery; a ban which Wesley endorsed with great conviction. However, Wesley chanced to observe slavery upon his visit to the colony of South Carolina. That experience with slavery prompted him to become zealously engaged in study about black Africa and the slave trade upon his return to England. That experience also caused him to become vigorously involved in a battle for the abolition of slavery—a battle which lasted for the rest of his life.

In 1743 when Wesley wrote the *General Rules*,[6] he had prohibited "the buying or selling the bodies and souls of men, women, and children, with an intention to enslave them." Throughout his ministry he was active in the antislavery campaign in England and threw all of his weight behind the efforts of William Wilberforce, Clarkson, Howard, and others to ban slavery throughout the British Empire.

Wesley's brief stay in Georgia was made shorter because of his opposition to the introduction of slavery into the Colony more than the affidavit sworn against him for barring "Miss Sophy" (Sophia Christiana Hopkey) from communion. Sophia Christiana Hopkey was the unmarried niece of a Mr. Causton, the chief magistrate of Savannah. Wesley, an unmarried clergyman, developed a deep friendship with her which eventuated into a love relationship. Some biographers of Wesley feel that there was "a perfectly benevolent conspiracy to promote a match between the two" on the part of Oglethorpe and others.[7] In any case, Sophia and Wesley did not make it to the altar together. After much agony and conflict over whether he should marry at all, and after seeking advice from several church leaders whom he trusted, Wesley broke off the relationship. Five days later, Wesley was informed by Sophia's aunt that Sophia was engaged to a Mr. Williamson, an unscrupulous landholder. She urged

---

[6] A document written by Wesley in which he outlined a guide to Christian ethics for Methodists. These rules were to be strictly followed by Methodists to exemplify their salvation.

[7] Cameron, *The Rise of Methodism. . . ,* pp. 109ff.

Wesley to speak to Sophia about the impending marriage, but Wesley stubbornly refused. Three days later Sophia Christiana Hopkey became Mrs. Williamson. Wesley then barred her from communion, insisting that she "own her fault and declare her repentance."

An affidavit was sworn out againt Wesley, accusing him of a misdemeanor by defaming the character of Sophia Williamson and "refusing to administer to her the Sacrament of the Lord's Supper in a public congregation, without cause."[8]

Those landowners who were angry with Wesley because of his opposition to the introduction of slavery into the Georgia Colony used this unfortunate confusion of wounded affection with pastoral duty to make Wesley's pastoral position in Georgia untenable.[9] Wesley did the only thing humanly possible under the circumstances. He shook the dust from his feet in Georgia and returned to England. But he did not give up his fight against slavery. Interestingly enough, George Whitefield, one of Wesley's early followers and preachers, did not scruple to buy some fifty slaves to work for the support of his orphan home—and this in spite of the fact that their use in the Colony had originally been forbidden by the Trustees. The answer to the perennial question about what to do with black people was already one that was not unanimous.

But Wesley furiously attacked slavery. His strategy was consistent with the rest of his ministry: an individual, direct appeal to the conscience of the guilty. In opposing slavery Wesley directly appealed to the captains of slaving ships, the dealers in slaves, and the slave-owners themselves. He was first and foremost an evangelist, and he relied primarily on the methods of evangelism to carry his antislavery message.

Although the Quakers had preceded him in their resolve in 1761 to disown all members who engaged in the slave traffic, Wesley was among the first to join the list against

[8]Wesley's *Journal* entry for August 8, 1737. *The Journal of the Rev. John Wesley, M.A.*, ed. Nehemiah Curnock (London: Epworth Press, 1938), Vol. I, p. 377.

[9]See Cameron, *The Rise of Methodism. . .* , pp. 89–91; 109–111; 120–121.

slavery. His "Thoughts Upon Slavery,"[10] written in 1774, has been assessed by many historians as the most far-reaching treatise ever written against slavery. It was widely distributed and reprinted in England and America. In this antislavery pamphlet Wesley reviled "the enslavement of the nobe by barbarous and inferior white men." He appealed to rationality and morality in addition to revelation to condemn slavery:

> But, waiving for the present all other consideration, I strike at the root of this complicated villainy. I absolutely deny all slave-holding to be consistent with any degree of natural justice, mercy, and truth. No circumstances can make it necessary for a man to burst in sunder all the ties of humanity. It can never be necessary for a rational being to sink himself below a brute. A man can be under no necessity of degrading himself into a wolf . . .
> Have you, has any man living, a right to use another as a slave? It cannot be, even setting Revelation aside. Liberty is the right of every human creature as soon as he breathes the vital air, and no human being can deprive him of that right which he derives from the law of nature.[11]

Although contemporary historians point out that the tract was really an abridgement of *Some Historical Account of Guinea*, published in Philadelphia in 1771 by the American Quaker, Anthony Benezet; the fact that Wesley circulated it under his name indicates that it represented his views. Besides, in eighteenth century England, such "borrowing" was common, and many circulated their colleagues' works to make them available to those who might not otherwise have seen them. It was a form of *endorsement*. In any case, the tract is consistent with Wesley's views expressed in other places: correspondence with the other leaders of the Society for the

---

[10]See Joseph Emory, ed., *The Works of the Rev. John Wesley, M.A.* (New York: Lane and Scott, 1850), Vol. I, p.

[11]John Wesley, "Thoughts Upon Slavery," quoted by Lucius C. Matlack, *The Anti-Slavery Struggle and Triumph in the Methodist Episcopal Church* (New York: Phillip and Hunt, 1881), pp. 40f.

Abolition of Slavery;[12] the sermon preached in 1788 in the city of Bristol, the stronghold of slave traders.[13]

The last letter that Wesley ever wrote, and perhaps his most famous, was addressed to William Wilberforce, the antislavery fighter, Member of Parliament and later, the Prime Minister of England. It was Wesley's last fervent appeal against slavery and a word to encourage Wilberforce to continue the fight against the enslavement of one human being by another. It is a passionate and eloquent plea:

> Dear Sir:
>
> Unless the divine power has raised you up to be as *Athanasius contra mundum*,[14] I see not how you can go through your glorious enterprise in opposing that execrable villainy which is the scandal of religion, of England, and of human nature. Unless God has raised you up for this very thing, you will be worn out by the opposition of men and devils. But if God be for you, who can be against you? Are all of them together stronger than God? O be not weary of well doing! Go on, in the name of God and in the power of his might, till even American slavery (the vilest that ever saw the sun) shall vanish away before it.
>
> Reading this morning a tract wrote by a poor African, I was particularly struck by that circumstance that a man who has a black skin, being wronged or outraged by a white man, can have no redress; it being a "law" in all our colonies that the *oath* of a black against a white goes for nothing. What villainy is this?[15]

Wesley was inalterably opposed to slavery and furiously attacked it. He saw it as an institution only to satisfy the greed of men. He denied that it was necessary in the eco-

[12]*The Letters of the Rev. John Wesley, M.A.*, ed., John Telford (London: The Epworth Press, 1931), Vol. 6.

[13]Maldwyn Edwards, *John Wesley and the Eighteenth Century: A Study of His Social and Political Influence* (New York: Abingdon Press, 1933), p. 120.

[14]"Athanasius arrayed against the world"; cf. R. Hooker, *Of the Laws of Ecclesiastical Politie* (1593–97), V, sec. 42.

[15]Cf. "Thoughts Upon Slavery;" see also Wesley's correspondence with the other leaders of the Society for the Abolition of Slavery in *Letters*, VIII, 6, 17, 23, 194, 207, 275.

nomic operation of the Colonies. And even if it were, he insisted that prosperity purchased at so great a price was an offense against God. From the initial view in South Carolina until the last letter on his death bed, Wesley believed that slavery was a deep-rooted evil that must be destroyed. And among other Methodists he created a strong antislavery sentiment and weaved it into the fabric of Wesleyan evangelism.

III

THE INCEPTION OF BLACK METHODISM: The Societies

Methodism came to America primarily through its Irish converts. Those young people whose hearts had been set aflame with the experiential form of faith characteristic of the Methodist conversion were anxious to spread it to America. It was simple, personal, and direct. There was very little liturgical or sacramental baggage—it required no mediation on the part of priests. It simply required a conviction of sin, a sense of guilt, faith in the divine forgiveness through the merits of Jesus Christ who died for sinners, and a feeling of justification or divine pardon for sin. This issued forth in a feeling of forgiveness with joy being the outward and inward manifestation of the spiritual transaction being completed. Wesley's experience at Aldersgate Street in 1738 in which he felt his heart "strangely warmed" was the archetype. Many Methodists told of having similar experiences, and witnessed to others about the glorious nature of this religious transformation and its accompanying assurance.

Robert Strawbridge, a native of Ulster in Ireland, had had such an experience, became a Methodist preacher, and journeyed to America on his own in the early sixties of the eighteenth century. He settled in the back country of Maryland on Sam's Creek in Frederick County and soon organized a Methodist Society in his home. John H. Graham points out that a joint commission, composed of representatives of the three precedent branches of the Methodist Church (Method-

15

ist Episcopal Church, the Methodist Protestant Church and the Methodist Episcopal Church South), after carefully surveying all of the available data, concluded that Strawbridge's Log Meeting House on Sam's Creek was where Methodism began its first society in America. On his tombstone in Mount Olivet Cemetery in Baltimore are inscribed the following words: "He built the Log Meeting House in Frederick County, Maryland, 1764, the first in America."[1]

The historical record reveals that blacks were among the charter members of that first Methodist Society. The roll of that first class includes the name of Anne Sweitzer, a slave named Anne of the Sweitzer family.[2] Unfortunately, we know little about her. But, unlike The Holy Nameless Two, we do know her name. Her name and her presence at that first class meeting, however, prove again that black Methodists were a part of Methodism in America from its inception. There can be no written history of Methodism in America without including those early pioneers who responded to the simple gospel message of the early Methodist preachers.

Black people were also present at the John Street Society of New York City when Phillip Embury, another native of Ireland, preached his first sermon. After Embury had been persuaded by Barbara Heck, his cousin, to hold the preaching service, he assembled a group of five persons in his home. Among his first worshippers was Betty, a black servant of the Heck household. They sang and prayed while Embury, a preacher licensed by Wesley, instructed them in the faith. From this meeting they formed themselves into a class, of which Embury became the leader. They resolved to attend regularly at his house for further instruction. By the end of

---

[1] See John H. Graham, *Black United Methodists* (New York: Vantage Press, 1979), pp. 10–11; Richard M. Cameron, *Methodism and Society in Historical Perspective* (Nashville: Abingdon Press, 1961), pp. 85–88; W. T. Watkins, *Out of Aldersgate* (Nashville: Department of Education of the Board of Missions of the Methodist Episcopal Church, South, 1937), pp. 48–49.

[2] *Ibid.*; See also Richardson, *op. cit.*, p. 284; Cameron, *Methodism and Society. . . ,* p. 87; Charles H. Wesley, *Richard Allen, Apostle of Freedom* (Washington: Associated Publishers, 1935), p. 40.

1776, the John Street Society had been established with Betty, the black servant of the Heck household, a charter member.[3] There were other blacks to follow, including Peter Williams who became an early black lay evangelist, and several other blacks who later formed the nucleus of those who separated from the John Street Church to form the African Methodist Episcopal Zion Church in 1796.

Even though a ladder stairway was to be built later to segregate the black and slave members into a gallery, two black women contributed to the funds to build Wesley Chapel (the first John Street). A. B. Hyde reports that

> Two hundred and fifty names of subscribers are still preserved, among which are African maids—Dinans and Chloes are in honor with the Livingstones and Delaneys, the blue blood of the time. Special mention must be made of Rachel, who gave nine shillings and Margaret contributed seven shillings.[4]

These early Methodist Societies saw black people respond to the powerfully dynamic and evangelistically-oriented gospel proclaimed by the Methodist preachers, and become a part of the Methodist movement as it took root in America. Some of these black converts themselves became powerful proclaimers of the gospel of Jesus Christ, sons of thunder and wielders of the "sledgehammer of truth beating on the iron heart of sin," as they sought to extend the Methodist movement and save people from the destruction of hell. We shall take a closer look at these brave and buoyant souls in a later chapter. But let it suffice here to say that from the very beginning of Methodism in America black people were a vital part of it. They heard the Methodists gladly and joined

---

[3] See "Black People and Their United Methodist Heritage," in *The Book of Discipline of the United Methodist Church* (Nashville: United Methodist Publishing House, 1976), pp. 14–15, hereafter referred to as simply *Discipline;* see Graham, p. 11; Cameron, *The Methodist Societies. . .* , pp. 86–87; Richardson, p. 35ff; and Bishop William A. Walls, *The African Methodist Episcopal Zion Church: Reality of the Black Church* (Charlotte, N.C.: A.M.E. Zion Publishing House, 1974), pp. 39ff.

[4] A. B. Hyde, *The Story of Methodism* (New York: M. W. Hazen Company, 1887), pp. 351–352.

the societies in Maryland and New York, Philadelphia and Long Island, and later other places where the simple gospel of the Methodists was proclaimed. In 1789, John Street Church reported 290 white members and 70 black members.[5] In 1787 St. George's Church in Philadelphia reported 270 white members and 17 black members.[6] The largest black membership reported in this period was the Calvert Circuit. It reported 505 white members and 342 blacks.[7] By 1786, ten years after the founding of the American nation, and only fourteen years since the founding of the first Methodist Society, and only four years after the formal founding of the Methodist Episcopal Church; there were 1,890 black members in the new denomination.[8] And, as has been shown, they gave of their meager earnings toward the establishment of a church. That church was later to wrestle with whether or not they could be truly Methodists. We must now consider in depth why black people responded to the preaching of the Methodist evangelists. What was the powerful appeal of Methodism to these black Americans?

---

[5] Walls, p. 41.
[6] W. C. Barclay, *History of Methodist Missions* (New York: Board of Missions and Church Extension), Vol. I, p. 268, cited by Graham, pp. 11–12.
[7] *Ibid.*
[8] *Ibid.*

IV

The Appeal of Methodism to Black Americans

There are numerous accounts of black Americans responding to the evangelistic message of the Methodists. Letters
were sent back to Wesley in England in abundance by the
preachers he sent to America. They told of the dramatic conversions of hundreds upon hundreds of blacks who accepted
Christianity in emotional and celebrative rejoicing. These
were sincere and profound religious experiences, as the
black slaves heard of a good and loving God who knew the
sufferings of his children, even his sun-baked sons and
daughters who found themselves in chains in a strange land.
Richard Allen, one of the early converts under Methodist
preaching and later the founder of the African Methodist
Episcopal Church, recorded some years later, his personal
conversation of 1777 typical of such dramatic conversions:

> . . . I was (he said) awakened and brought to see myself,
> poor, wretched and undone, and without the mercy of God
> must be lost. Shortly after, I obtained mercy through the
> blood of Christ, and was constrained to exhort my old com-
> panions to seek the Lord. I went rejoicing for several days and
> was happy in the Lord, in conversing with many old, experi-
> enced Christians. I was brought under doubts, and was
> tempted to believe I was deceived, and was constrained to
> seek the Lord afresh. I went with my head bowed down for
> many days. My sins were a heavy burden. I was tempted to
> believe there was no mercy for me. I cried to the Lord both
> night and day. One night I thought hell would be my portion.

I cried unto Him who delighteth to hear the prayers of a poor sinner, and all of a sudden my dungeon shook, my chains flew off, and, glory to god, I cried. My soul was filled. I cried, enough for me—the Saviour died. Now my confidence was strengthened that the Lord, for Christ's sake, had heard my prayers and pardoned all my sins.[1]

On November 4, 1769, Richard Boardman wrote to John Wesley telling of the blacks attending his meetings and how their response affected him:

Our house contains about seven hundred people. About a third part of those who attend get in, the rest are glad to hear without. There appears such a willingness in the Americans to hear the word as I never saw before. They have no preaching in some parts of the back settlements. I doubt not but an effectual door will be opened among them. O! May the Most High give his Son the heathen for his inheritance. The number of blacks that attend the preaching affects me much.[2]

And as blacks became members of the new Methodist movement they became faithful in their devotions and sincere in their commitment to worship. Abel Stevens describes how one such incident led to the conversion of the plantation owner:

Henry D. Gough, wealthy planter, heard Asbury preach. He was deeply impressed and burdened. He could no longer enjoy his accustomed pleasures.

He became deeply serious and, at last melancholy, and was near destroying himself under the awakened sense of his misspent life; but God mercifully preserved him. Riding to one of his plantations, he heard the voice of prayer and praise in a cabin, and, listening, discovered that a negro from a neighboring estate was leading the devotions of his own slaves, and offering fervent thanksgivings for the blessings of their depressed lot. His heart was touched, and with emotion he exclaimed, "Alas, O Lord, I have my thousands and tens of thousands, and yet, ungrateful wretch that I am, I never thanked thee, as this poor slave does, who has scarcely

---

[1]Richard Allen, *The Life Experience and Gospel Labors of the Rt. Rev. Richard Allen* (Nashville: Abingdon Press, 1960), 2nd Edition, pp. 15–16.

[2]Letter to John Wesley, quoted in Abel Stevens, *History of the Methodist Church* (New York: Carlton and Porter, 1866), Vol. I, p. 103.

clothes to put on or food to satisfy his hunger." The luxurious master was taught a lesson, on the nature of true contentment and happiness, which he could never forget. His work-worn servants in their lowly cabins knew a blessedness which he had never found in his sumptuous mansion.[3]

The *Discipline* of the United Methodist Church attempts to account for the response of black Americans to Methodism. In its discussion of "Black People and Their United Methodist Heritage," it asserts the following:

Methodism won favor with the black people for two main reasons: (1) its evangelistic appeal; (2) the Church's attitude toward slavery.[4]

While these two reasons are certainly true in summary, and merit further explanation, there were some other factors that also need to be included.

A SINCERE AND SIMPLE MESSAGE: A CALL TO RIGHTEOUSNESS

The Wesleyan evangelical message was a simple gospel of salvation, designed to awaken a godly experience in its hearers of a conscious fellowship with God. Emphasizing the love of God and the way of redemption, it sought to bring into the lives of poor benighted sinners the message of a Father who cares for his children—all of his children. This conscious acceptance with God issues forth in daily growth in holiness. Christians have as their dominant motives the love of God and of their neighbor, and these could free them from sin. Poverty was no barrier to membership; the poorest were made most welcome. Religion, for these early Wesleyans, was not a perfunctory, ritualistic faith, but rather an "experience" of faith through which one responded to the love of God. It was a clarion call to righteousness in this world in order to escape eternal damnation in the world to come.

These evangelists never left their hearers and congrega-

[3] *Ibid.*, p. 236f.
[4] *Discipline*, p. 15.

tions with any doubts about the living reality of the divine mercy. In almost every sermon this eternal mercy was assured; it was sung in the Charles Wesley and Isaac Watts hymns; the theme ran like music through all occasions. Even though hell in all of its terrors was graphically pictured, the preachers never forgot to proclaim the offer of divine mercy that was "wider than the sea." The sufferings of hell were made realistic in order to make the way of salvation even more glorious.

The Wesleyan revivalists were Arminian in theology as opposed to strict Calvinism. They held that Christ died for all, that salvation is by faith alone, that those who believe are saved, that those who reject God's grace are lost, and that God does not elect particular individuals for either outcome. Strict Calvinism held that before God had created the world He had decreed who should be saved and who should be damned in a kind of pre-election. It was over this issue that Wesley and Whitefield split and this perhaps accounts for their differences on the issue of slavery. Whitefield was a strict Calvinist who believed in predestination. Obviously, for Whitefield, God had not elected black people and therefore they could easily serve as slaves and be the hewers of the wood and drawers of the water now henceforth and forever. Whitefield provided the spurious and devastating theological and biblical bases for slavery out of his Calvinism, as well as maintained slaves as we have seen earlier.

The Arminian tradition, however, prevailed in its emphasis upon prevenient grace, i.e., that God bestows will as well as the grace that is willed, and that grace is sufficient to effectually impel belief. The Methodists preached such a grace that breaks every barrier down.

As Walter G. Muelder points out, there was in this simple message a revolutionary potential for the unwanted poor and uninterested destitute who were excluded through social stratification from the "morally soft and spiritually dead churches of the well to do." It is evident in one of the now-famous letters of the Duchess of Buckingham to Lord Huntington:

> Their doctrines (those of the Methodist preachers) are most repulsive and tinctured with impertinence and disrespect toward their superiors, in perpetually endeavoring to level all ranks and doing away with all distinctions. It is monstrous to be told that you have a heart as sinful as the common wretches that crawl the earth. This is highly offensive and insulting.[5]

Blacks were attracted to such a simplistic and sincere message, as were the poor white farmers, and those who were the outcasts and the declassé masses. Great numbers flocked to hear this good news, and expressed their feelings with cries, screams, shouts, tears, prostrations, physical convulsions, and other physical and emotional responses, including sometimes falling insensibly.

John Thompson, born as a slave in Maryland in 1812, draws the clear distinction between this revivalist preaching and the more ritualistic and staid approach of the established church:

> My mistress and her family were all Episcopalians. The nearest church was five miles from our plantation and there was no Methodist church nearer than ten miles. So we went to the Episcopal Church, but always came home as we went, for the preaching was above our comprehension, so we could understand but little that was said. But soon the Methodist religion was brought among us, and preached in a manner so plain that the wayfaring man, though a fool, could not err therein. This new doctrine produced great consternation among the slaveholders. It was something which they could not understand. It brought glad tidings to the poor bondsman; it bound up the broken-hearted; it opened the prison doors to them that were bound, and let the captives go free. As soon as it got among the slaves, it spread from plantation to plantation, until it reached ours, where there were but few who did not experience religion.[6]

---

[5] Quoted by Walter G. Muelder in "Methodism's Contribution to Social Reform," *Methodism*, ed. by William K. Anderson (Nashville: The Methodist Publishing House, 1947), p. 193.

[6] John Thompson, *The Life of John Thompson, A Fugitive Slave* (Worcester, Mass., 1856), pp. 18–19. Quoted by Albert J. Raboteau, *Slave Religion* (New York: Oxford University Press, 1980), p. 133.

THE EARLY OPPOSITION TO SLAVERY

Second, the slaves responded to the Methodists because these early evangelists were opposed to slavery. John Wesley's uncompromising stance against slavery has been shown earlier. But Thomas Coke, Francis Asbury, Freeborn Garrettson and most of the early Methodist evangelists— with the notable exception of George Whitefield—were opposed to slavery. This eventuated in seventeen Methodist ministers at a conference in Baltimore taking up the question of slavery and deciding that itinerant preachers holding slaves had to promise to set them free. They declared "slavery is contrary to the laws of God, man and nature—hurtful to society; contrary to the dictates of conscience and pure religion, and doing that which we would not others should do to us and ours." This was not the end of Methodists' dealing with slavery and the question of blacks. We shall discuss further the Methodist Church and slavery in a succeeding section. But let it suffice here to say that Methodism began in America with its leadership opposed to slavery and was evangelical in that stance—to which the slaves earnestly responded.

Harry V. Richardson points out the fact that "despite their enslaved condition, the blacks came in large numbers to attend the meetings, hear the Gospel, and seek conversion [it] made all the more poignant the inhumanity of slavery and the sin of it."[7] Asbury found himself moved by the antislavery leadership of the Quakers to write in his Journal in 1778: "I find the most pious part of the people called Quakers, are exerting themselves for the liberation of the slaves. This is a very laudable design; and what the Methodists must come to, or, I fear the Lord will depart from them."[8] Freeborn Garrettson upon his conversion in 1777 is reported

---

[7] Richardson, *op. cit.*, p. 52.
[8] See Mathews, Donald G. Slavery on Methodism.

to have immediately emancipated his slaves on religious grounds. He declared that it was God, not man, who showed him the impropriety of holding slaves, and he joined the ranks of those early Methodist preachers who fought slavery.

Perhaps the clearest evidence of how the slaves felt about the Methodists and their stance on slavery is seen in the account of the Gabriel Prosser slave revolt. Prosser, convinced on religious grounds—perhaps the influence of the evangelical Methodists—that slavery should be overturned and that he had been chosen by God to be a deliverer of his people, planned a rebellion. A young man of twenty-five with impressive physical and mental capabilities, and also a student of the Bible, Gabriel felt that he was to follow the model of Samson against the Philistines. Perhaps this possibility seemed even more likely to him in 1800. Toussaint L'Ouverture had recently completed a successful revolution against slavery in Haiti and had taken command of the entire colony of Santo Domingo. Gabriel's plan was to destroy Henrico County and lead the slaves to the establishment of a new black kingdom in Virginia, with himself to be crowned king. The plan called for killing all the whites who accosted his followers, seizing arms and ammunition from the arsenal in nearby Richmond, looting the treasury and, if possible, arriving at an agreement with the remaining slavemasters for the freedom of all slaves. It was a well-planned plot in which Gabriel's testimony declared he had ten thousand men ready to go into battle. The insurrection failed because of logistical problems, slave informers, and a serious storm. Gabriel and a number of other slaves were hanged. But Gabriel's instructions concerning the two Christian groups he believed to be on God's side against the practice of slavery were clear: *All Methodists and Quakers were to be spared.* He also included Frenchmen, presumably because France had recognized the new nation L'Ouverture had established on the island of Hispaniola.

Clearly, Gabriel knew of the Methodist witness against

slavery. Some would maintain that it was through the itinerant ministers who went back and forth from church to church that information was transmitted to the insurgents.[9]

THE APPEAL TO EMOTION: THE PREACHER, HIS STYLE, AND HIS MESSAGE

In addition to black Americans responding because of the evangelical, simple message of salvation of the Methodists, and the attitudes of the early Methodist leaders toward slavery, there are at least three other factors that account for the appeal of Methodism to black Americans. These are: (1) the preaching and worship style of the Methodists appealed to blacks; (2) blacks were allowed to serve as lay preachers; and (3) Methodism was adaptable enough to fit their own unique situation so that they could make it their own.

The major stress of the evangelistic Methodists as well as the Baptists and, perhaps to a lesser degree, the Presbyterians, was on the conversion experience itself. While the Methodists had a concern that the conversion experience ought to issue forth in daily growth in holiness and Christian conduct, even "moving on toward perfection" *after* the conversion, it was the *experience* of conviction, repentance and regeneration which primarily occupied the attention of the preacher. The more established clergymen of the Anglican Church tended to concentrate on moralizing and teaching doctrines. Their preaching style reflected this didactic preoccupation. They were concerned that the slaves learn to recite the Ten Commandments and the Lord's Prayer and the Apostle's Creed. They expected the slaves to be able to give the correct answers to the catechismal questions. One of the missionaries for the Society for the Propagation of the Gospel in Foreign Parts gives us an account of this emphasis:

> Upon these gentlewomen's desiring me to come and examine these negroes . . . I went and among other things I asked them, Who Christ was. They readily answered, He is the Son

[9]See Gayraud Wilmore's discussion of this point in *Black Religion and Black Radicalism* (Garden City, N.Y.: Anchor Press, 1973), pp. 77ff.

of God, and Savior of the World, and told me that they embraced Him with all their hearts as such, and I desired them to rehearse the Apostle's Creed and the 10 Commandments and the Lord's Prayer, which they did very distinctly and perfectly. 14 of them gave me so great satisfaction, and were so desirous to be baptized, that I thought it my duty to baptize them and therefore baptized these 14 last Lord's Day. And I doubt not but these gentlewomen will prepare the rest of them for Baptisme in a little time.[10]

But the evangelical Methodist preacher was primarily concerned about the experience of conversion, and exhorted the slave by visualizing, personalizing, and dramatizing the nature of sin and salvation to picture the darkness of sin and the glorious light of salvation. He helped them to see the beauty of the Father seeking after the son who is the prodigal. He helped them to feel the weight of sin, to picture in their minds the threats of hell, and to accept Christ as their only Savior. Like an artist, he drew a picture on the canvas of the minds of the hearers. This was an emotional and appealing word for the converted heart; a reminder of the day and hour when "the dungeon shook and the chains flew off." And it filled their hearts with gladness and rejoicing. For those who had never heard the message of salvation, it made the soul feel happy as they "came out of de wilderness, leaning on de Lord." These preachers' style was dictated both by the message and an overriding passionate goal: to help the poor sinner make a decision for heaven rather than allow their souls to be consigned to hell. And the preachers exhorted this fiery message of salvation and hope with personal, emotional appeal, and enthusiasm that often triggered responses of infectious groans and shouts which spread throughout the meeting place. It was not just the message but also the manner in which it was delivered.

Thomas Rankin, one of the revivalists, reports his experience on the Baltimore Circuit:

[10]Quoted in *Classified Digest of the Records of the Society for the Propagation of the Gospel in Foreign Parts* (London: 1893), p. 16. Cited by E. Franklin Frazier, *The Negro in the United States* (New York: The Macmillan Co., 1949), p. 337.

Near the close of the meeting I stood up and called upon the people to look toward that part of the chapel where all the blacks were. I then said, "See the number of Africans who have stretched out their hands unto God!" While I was addressing the people thus, it seemed as if the very house shook with the mighty power and glory of Sinai's God. Many of the people were so overcome that they were ready to faint and die under his Almighty hand. For about three hours the gale of the Spirit thus continued to breathe upon the dry bones; and they did live the life of glorious love! As for myself, I scarce knew whether I was in the body or not; and so it was with all my brethren . . . Surely the fruits of this season will remain to all eternity.[11]

As Raboteau comments, "the revivalists, moreover, tended to minimize complex explanations of doctrines. The heightened emphasis on conversion left little room for elaborate catechesis."[12] For their spiritual nurture the converts were organized into "Societies" and these were subdivided into "classes" with a "class leader." This was part of the organizational genius of Wesley. With such minimal organization, slaves could be taken into the movement and fully participate more easily than in a settled and established church. It must be remembered that Wesley's interest was not to start a new church, but a drive for renewal, revival, and piety within the established church. (However, these Societies did become churches in the fullest sense in 1784, when Thomas Coke was dispatched by John Wesley, over the objections of his brother Charles, to form the new church.)

The other aspect of the worship which attracted and appealed to the slaves involved the singing. The Methodists became known for their vigorous and spirited singing of hymns and psalms. John Wesley had emphasized singing from the very beginning of the movement. He was a hymn writer himself and translated some of the early hymns of the German reformers and the early church into English. During

---

[11] Stevens, *op. cit.*, p. 44.
[12] Raboteau, p. 133.

his brief stay in America, his volume, *A Collection of Psalms and Hymns,* published in Charlestown, South Carolina in 1737, became one of the first hymnals in the English language prepared for use in public worship.[13] His concern for the publishing and singing of hymns continued until his death. Before breathing his last breath, he is said to have sung one of his favorite hymns: "I'll Praise My Maker While I've Breath."

In Wesley's preface to *Sacred Melody* in 1761 he developed some seven specific directions for singing, which are printed in the current *Methodist Hymnal.* One of these admonishes the Methodists: "Sing lustily and with good courage. Beware of singing as if you were half dead, or half asleep; but lift up your voice with strength. Be no more afraid of your voice now, no more ashamed of its being heard, than when you sung the songs of Satan."

But it was really Charles Wesley who was the poet and hymn-writer of Methodism. In all, he wrote more than six thousand hymns, many of which are among the great hymns of the Christian Church. He is considered by most hymnologists, in both quantity and quality alike, the great hymn writer of all ages. He is rivaled only by Isaac Watts, the dissenter of the previous century, who had become the father of the modern hymns by setting the metrical Psalms to poetical form. But Charles Wesley's body of works would carry many more of the favorite hymns which became part of the heart and center of the Methodist worship, and would account for the popularity and the appeal of Methodism to the black slaves. It also revolutionized the concept of worship and influenced the camp meetings and the revivals which blossomed into the Second Great Awakening. The circuit riders carried a simple message of the gospel and an informal service of worship, consisting primarily of extem-

[13]See "Preface" to *The Methodist Hymnal* (Nashville: The Methodist Publishing House, 1964), p. v.

porary preaching, prayer, and hymn-singing, across the fields and plains of America and into the backwoods and towns and hamlets.

There was something in the vigorous singing of the hymns of the Methodists that awakened a familiarity to the Africans, perhaps half-forgotten while half-remembered, but nevertheless still there, in the recesses of their being. Even with the absence of African gods and the replacement of the Christian God, the African heritage of singing was brought back to mind by the Methodist meetings. The ancient African dictum, "the spirit will not descend without song," was made manifest. And, "the still white notes of the Wesleyan Hymnal"[14] notwithstanding, it was a far cry from the Gregorian chants and plainsong.

Francis Asbury commented that the African slaves sang "in cheerful melody."[15] Perhaps it was the sound of their kinsmen joining in song that would lead hundreds of slaves to the sites of these evangelical meetings. The Rev. Greene gives a detailed description of how the hymn-singing spread into the cultural life of the black slave quarters:

> At night, especially in the summer time, after everybody had eaten supper, it was common thing for us to sit outside. The old folks would get together and talk until bedtime. Sometimes somebody would start humming an old hymn, and then the next-door neighbor would pick it up. In this way it would finally get around to every house, and then the music started. Soon everybody would be gathered together, and such singing! It wouldn't be long before some of the slaves got happy and started to shouting . . .[16]

It is, therefore, not surprising that Charles A. Tindley, a former slave and Methodist pastor of East Calvary Methodist Episcopal Church of Philadelphia (now changed to Tindley Temple in honor of him) for more than thirty years served as

---

[14] A pejorative description of the Wesleyan hymn often used by Imanu Amiri Baraka (LeRoi Jones).

[15] See Richardson, *op. cit.*, p. 48.

[16] *God Struck Me Dead* (Philadelphia: Pilgrim Press, 1969), pp. 87–88.

a prolific writer of gospel hymns and the forerunner and father of modern gospel music.[17] His songs became a "profound universal appeal to the human heart with words of hope, cheer, love and pity." Commenting on the contribution of this one-time slave and hod carrier, Dr. J. Jefferson Cleveland comments: "He bequeathed to all Methodism and to Christianity a legacy that will live on through his hymns."[18]

Another significant reason why blacks were attracted to Methodism was the fact that slaves were, early in the movement, allowed to preach and were licensed as local preachers and later as travelling preachers. As opposed to the Presbyterians, Congregationalists, Disciples, Lutherans, Episcopalians, Moravians and other mainline Protestant denominations, Baptist and Methodist churches had black preachers. There was an exception here and there; for example, the Presbyterians licensed George M. Erskine, a slave in east Tennessee in 1818; and Hiram Revels, later to be elected to the United States Senate, left the A.M.E. Church to organize a Presbyterian Church in St. Louis in 1855 which was subsequently closed.

If the slave had a converted heart and a gifted tongue and showed talent for exhorting, he exhorted, and not merely to black congregations. We shall discuss in the next section that elite group of black Methodist preachers, including "Black Harry" Hoosier, who travelled with Bishop Francis Asbury; Henry Evans, a free-born black of Virginia, who is credited with establishing Methodism among both blacks and whites in Fayetteville, North Carolina; and John Stewart, who ministered in Ohio among the Wyandotte Indians and gave birth to the home missions enterprise in the Methodist Church.

Raboteau points out that among the Methodists many black men served as lay preachers: "They could not celebrate

---

[17] He is described as the "father of gospel music" by Thomas A. Dorsey and the late Mahalia Jackson, a modern gospel singer.

[18] See J. Jefferson Cleveland, ed., *Songs of Zion* (Nashville: Abingdon Press, 1981), pp. 4–6.

the sacraments [nor could white lay preachers], but were allowed to preach and discipline black members within a certain locale."[19] Even when the laws were passed forbidding such a practice, the Methodists sent out black assistants with their itinerant preachers. The Methodists skirted the law by creating a preaching category, "exhorters." In the strictest sense, black exhorters were really black preachers. And these so-called "exhorters" were known to act as pastors of their own people.[20]

Few have really assessed and appreciated the importance of these black preachers for the conversion of slaves to Christianity, and the spread of Methodism among both blacks and whites. Following the Revolutionary War and into the early decades of the next century, they became the critical link between Christian belief and the experiential world of the slaves. It was these black preachers who saved their souls and sanity with their interpretation of the humanity of God's children and the fatherhood of God. They gave realism and substance to things hoped for and a taste of things not seen. The preacher was a part of the travails of the people, for whatever happened to the people happened to him also. Wherever they were, he was there, too . . . kneeling on the cold dirt floor of a slave hut . . . picking cotton in the long, hot, dusty and endless rows . . . making his way along the long and lonely wilderness trails to get to his church and his people to fulfill his calling and keep his charge. He stood between the inexhaustible storehouse of hope and the depleted lives of his beleaguered and bewildered flock, and shouted a word to keep them going: "Walk together, children! Don't get weary!" And he preached a fiery gospel with a pastor's heart and proclaimed himself a steward of a mystery that offered to the oppressed slaves salvation and hope, and an escape from earthly woes.

[19] Raboteau, *op. cit.*, p. 136.

[20] See Donald G. Matthews, *Slavery and Methodism: A Chapter in American Morality, 1780–1845* (Princeton: Princeton University Press, 1965), pp. 64ff. Also see his explanatory notes in *ibid*.

A correspondent to Georgia expressed her amazement at the eloquence of these preachers to the editor of the *American Missionary:*

> I listened to a remarkable sermon or talk a few evenings since. The preacher spoke of the need for atonement for sin. "Bullocks c'dn't do it, heifers c'dn't do it, de blood of doves c'dn't do it—but up in heaven, for thousan and thousan of years, the Son was saying to the Father, 'Put up a soul, put up a soul. Prepare me a body, an I will go an meet Justice on Calvary's brow!'" He was so dramatic. In describing the crucifixion he said: "I see the sun when she turned herself black. I see the stars a fallin from the sky, and them old Herods comin out of their graves and goin about the city, an they knew 'twas the Lord's Glory."[21]

But the black slaves who heard these preachers often were accustomed to such eloquence, and preferred its experiential, dramatic and picturesque message. They responded to him and his message with tears of sorrow and shouts of joy and committed lives. They were converted in great numbers, and black congregations sprang up wherever they were allowed.

A REFASHIONED CHRISTIANITY

It is at this critical juncture that a bicultural synthesis begins to take place. The Afro-American culture has its beginning as these black leaders nurture the birth of these Christian communities and become the initiators and prime movers of a culture that persists unto this day.

The University of Chicago sociologist, the late Robert Park, has commented on these men and their movement:

> With the appearance of these men, the Negroes in America ceased to be a mission people. At least from this time on, the movement went on its own momentum, more and more largely under the direction of Negro leaders. Little Negro congregations, under the leadership of Negro preachers, sprang

---

[21] *American Missionary,* 8 (April, 1864), p. 100. Quoted in Raboteau, p. 235.

up wherever they were tolerated. Often they were suppressed, more often they were privately encouraged. Not infrequently they met in secret.[22]

Methodism was extended and black people responded to it in greater numbers because of these black sons of thunder who moved across the pages of history almost unnoticed by historians, but who made an indelible impression on the lives of black people and thus began a continuing line of faith and splendor. And this new breed refashioned the Christian faith through their genius for exhortation.

Before looking at the third factor in black people's response to Methodism, a word must be said about how the hierarchical structure viewed these men. Even though a number of black preachers served regular stations and circuits as well as in missions, and were licensed as exhorters and local preachers, there were severe limitations. They were licensed by the Quarterly Conferences and had no voice in their own annual renewal, nor did they vote for one another. As John Dixon Long, a white Methodist minister, put it: "Even in the midst of their brethren, they are made to feel they are not one in Christ Jesus."[23] Determinative control and power lay far beyond the reach of these men whose flaming ambition was to be faithfully about their errands as good servants of Jesus Christ.

The third factor contributing to black involvement in and response to Methodism was that it was adaptable enough to their own situation so that they could make it their own. They refashioned the Christian tradition as introduced by the zealous Methodists into a religion that served their needs and their victimized situation. E. Franklin Frazier, in his penetrating study of *The Negro in America*, accounts for this factor:

[22]Robert E. Park, "The Conflict and Fusion of Cultures with Special Reference to the Negro," *Journal of Negro History*, Vol 4, No. 2 (April, 1919), p. 120.

[23]E. A. Andrews, *Slavery and the Domestic Slave-Trade in the United States* (Boston: 1836), p. 37. Quoted in Raboteau, p. 207.

But there were even more fundamental psychological factors in human nature which offer an explanation of the response of the slaves to the religion of the Methodists and Baptists. The slaves, who had been torn from their homeland, from family and friends, and whose cultural heritage had disintegrated or had lost its meaning in a new environment, were broken men. The bonds of a common tradition, of religious beliefs and practices, had been broken and the Negroes had become "atomized" in the American environment. Here was an appeal, emotional and simple, that provided a new way of life and drew them into a union at first with whites, but later formed a stronger bond with members of their own race.[24]

Without yielding Frazier's analysis in total that the Africans were completely "atomized,"[25] there is adequate evidence suggesting that the new religion created a bond of social cohesion and influenced what develops. But what emerged from the creative genius of these African slaves who became Methodists and Baptists is not merely a replica of the white religion nor the white church. It is a dual process in which the blacks accept Christianity and its peculiar evangelical interpretation and, at the same time, make it their own. They did not merely become Christians; they created a faith that met their own needs as blacks experiencing a particular kind of oppression in America.[26] They fashioned a Christian tradition to fit their own situation.

One can even say they fashioned something new in the same sense that Shakespeare's plays were new. Shakespeare's themes and plots were not "new," for almost all of

[24]Frazier, *op. cit.*, p. 339.

[25]Raboteau's discussion, summary and evaluation of the age-old Herskovits-Frazier debate is refreshingly illuminating. See Raboteau, pp. 48ff.

[26]See Gayraud S. Wilmore, *Black Religion and Black Radicalism* (Garden City, N.Y.: Anchor Press, 1973), pp. 1–19; Raboteau, *op. cit.*, pp. 152–210, especially pp. 207–210. Peter J. Paris has a well-developed argument that there is a distinct "Black Christian Tradition" that has developed in America "as a non-racist appropriation of the Christian faith" which challenges racism in all spheres of its influence: social, religious, moral. See his essay, "The Moral and Political Significance of the Black Churches in America" in *Belief and Ethics: Essays in Honor of Alvin Pitcher* (Chicago: Center for Scientific Study of Religion, 1977), pp. 315–329.

his stories were borrowed from chronicles, biography, prose tale or Greek myths and tales. But the way that they were weaved together and expressed was new. For he unerringly seized upon the dramatic elements and revealed life in its full richness and movement. Likewise, what the black Methodists did with the western Christian religion was to take on the outward appearance of Christian conversion, and take from it whatever was efficacious for easing their burdens in captivity, whatever offered hope in facing their earthly woes; and they seized its prophetic tradition for moral reform in a specific societal context and paid little attention to the rest.

The difference was not always apparent to the slave-master, nor even to the white evangelical preachers and missionaries. A white Methodist minister who had preached to black Methodists at Charleston belatedly discovered the dichotomy and reflected this new knowledge in his report:

> There were near fourteen hundred colored communicants . . . (Their) service was always thronged—galleries, lower floor, chancel, pulpit, steps and all . . . The preacher could not complain of any deadly space between himself and congregation. He was positively breast up to his people, with no possible loss of . . . rapport. Though ignorant of it at the time, he remembers now the cause of the enthusiasm under his deliverances (about) the 'law of liberty' and 'freedom from Egyptian bondage.' What was figurative they interpreted literally. He thought of but one ending of the war; they quite another. He remembers the sixty-eight Psalm as affording numerous texts for their declaration, e.g., 'Let God arise, let his enemies be scattered'; His 'march through the wilderness'; 'The Chariots of God are twenty thousand'; 'The hill of God is as the hill of Basham'; and especially, 'Though ye have lain among the pots, yet shall ye be as the wings of a dove covered with silver, and her feathers with yellow gold' . . . It is mortifying now to think that his comprehension was not equal to the African intellect. All he thought about was relief from the servitude of sin, and freedom from the bondage of the devil . . . But they interpreted it literally in the good time coming,

which of course could not but make their ebony complexion attractive, very.[27]

The black Methodists may have been, by and large, un-educated, but they were not fools. They knew that a religion which talked about justice and righteousness and oneness in Christ, yet failed to ordain their brothers and husbands, and insulted the black Christians by seating them in separate areas, and oppressed the black sons and daughters of a just God by forcing them to remain slaves had something wrong with it. It had to be re-interpreted and refashioned to meet their needs. There was nothing wrong with the message: there was something wrong with both the messengers and those who sat in the choicest seats.

[27] A. M. Chreitzberg, *Early Methodism in the Carolinas* (Nashville: Methodist Book Concern, 1897), pp. 158–159.

V

BLACK SONS OF THUNDER:
Three Exemplary Evangels

The early years of Methodism in America and its rapid growth yielded many black converts to the Christian faith. The circuit rider stands as one of the major contributors to this phenomenal spread. Astride his horse, he crossed the frontier, bringing the gospel to an essentially untrodden, yet rapidly burgeoning America. In America in the late eighteenth century and early nineteenth century, the wilderness was almost unending; there was the log cabin, the small farm, the remote plantation, the isolated family. But the circuit rider was on the move, keeping pace with the population, riding into hamlets where more than likely no church existed, preaching on plantations in Virginia, Maryland, the Carolinas and Georgia. He preached in brush arbors, on country store porches, in clapboard meeting houses, and clearings down beside the mountain streams. At whatever preaching place, the slaves gathered to hear him and respond.

Booker T. Washington, in *The Story of the Negro in America*, published in 1909, surveyed the long, arduous struggle of slavery and the part played by these mounted circuit riders sent out by John Wesley: "The Negro seems from the beginning to have been very closely associated with the Methodist Church in the United States. Methodism had started in England among the poor and the outcast; it was natural, there-

39

fore, that when its missionaries came to America they should seek to bring into the Church the outcast and neglected people, especially the slaves."

Some of these slaves converted to Methodism became powerful preachers of the gospel they had heard and felt. After their "dungeons shook" and their "chains fell off," their "stammering tongues were loosened" to testify to others of the wretchedness of sin and the glory of salvation found in the Savior who died. They became "sons of thunder" and their words "sledge hammers of truth, beating on the iron heart of sin" in the souls of those who were unredeemed, and especially in the souls of the black diaspora of the West African motherland.

It was no simple task to which they set their hands. It was a backbreaking, heartbreaking, often dehumanizing and dangerous time for a black man to be a preacher. He faced opposition both subtle and blatant. And regardless of his status—slave or free—there was always the white master with whom he had to contend. Reprisals could be swift and painful. Being a black preacher at the beginning of Methodism required remarkable courage, tact and finesse, adapting a philosophy of "being wise as serpents and harmless as doves." These black preachers were required to be faithful to the gospel while they proclaimed a message of hope to an oppressed people caught in an inconceivable social situation. It called for complete dedication to sustain their ministries through all the vagaries of weather, tortuous trails along dense woodlands, and sometimes hostile crowds and communities, as these weary travellers made their way to the people to thunder the good news that grace was available to all.

These heroic forebears of black Methodist preachers made an inestimable contribution to the development and establishment of the Methodist Church. We shall look at the lives and contributions of three of these elite black sons of thunder.

"BLACK HARRY" HOOSIER: A HORSEMAN FOR THE LORD

Harry Hoosier,[1] or "Black Harry" as he was called, became a circuit rider and a travelling companion to several of the best-known preachers of Methodism at the latter part of the eighteenth century. W. H. Daniels, a prominent Methodist historian of more than a century ago, said: "At different times (Black Harry) acted as driver for the carriage of Asbury, Coke, Whatcoat, and Garrettson; but he excelled all of his masters in popularity as a preacher."[2]

Inasmuch as Harry Hoosier could neither read nor write, there are no personal records or journals from his own hand—no sermons, papers, or letters. Much of what we know of him comes through oral tradition, stories, legends and references made to him by those who knew him personally. Thus, we see him through the eyes of others—those who travelled with him and heard him preach. Asbury mentions him in his *Journal* nine times. Freeborn Garrettson records his impressions of and experiences with Harry Hoosier in his writings; and Coke makes several references to him in his *Journal*. He is reported to be the first Methodist preacher, white or black, to be commented upon in a New York newspaper, *The New York Packet*.

The Rev. Joshua E. Licorish, a retired pastor of Zoar Church in Philadelphia whose avocation is Black Methodist history, has for many years collected material on Harry Hoosier. African Zoar Methodist Episcopal Church is the oldest continuing black congregation of the United Methodist Church in America.[3] Licorish credits Harry Hoosier with

[1] There are several different spellings in the accounts of "Black Harry:" Hosier, Hoshur, Hossier. The spelling Hoosier shall be used throughout unless quoted material uses a different spelling.

[2] Quoted in an unpublished paper by John W. Coleman, "Heroic Black Figures of Early Methodism," 1981, p. 7.

[3] St. Paul United Methodist Church in Oxon Hill, Maryland, makes the claim that it is older than African Zoar. It purports to date back to 1791. During the recent celebration of its 190th anniversary, a published history made the following state-

the founding of Zoar. It was composed of those blacks who remained at St. George's Church after Richard Allen, Absalom Jones, and others left because of racial illtreatment. Zoar's first lot was purchased and the first edifice built in 1794. Bishop Asbury records that it was opened on Thursday, August 4, 1796—strangely, he does not mention Harry Hoosier in his entry.

It is unfortunate that "he who first introduced Methodism to the eloquence, passion, and fire of black preaching"[4] left us no record of his sermons and his life. But his reputation as preacher becomes even more marvelous when it is recognized that this unlettered son of thunder who travelled with the learned Dr. Thomas Coke and the pioneering Bishop Francis Asbury was more popular than they. It is reported that when someone inquired about his illiteracy he replied: "I sing by faith, pray by faith, and do every thing by faith; without faith in Jesus Christ I can do nothing."[5]

Many of those who have written about Harry Hoosier assume that he was born near Fayetteville, North Carolina, about 1750. He is described physically as being "small in stature, and coal black, and had eyes of remarkable brilliancy

---

ment: "The original organization of this society of Negro adherents (St. Paul) was apparently preached to by Ezekiel Cooper, 1763–1847. The records show that in October 1791—'I preached to a small congregation the evening being rainy but few attended—between one and two hundred. Thursday 10 I went over the Potomac and preached in Oxenhill in a small preaching house which has been built by a number of religious black people. I had considerable satisfaction among them. I preached at 12 o'clock again at night. The dear black people seem to be alive to God having their hearts placed on things above.' ("History of St. Paul United Methodist Church," *We've Come This Far By Faith* (Oxon Hill, Md.: St. Paul Press, 1981), p. 15.) Several questions must be raised: Did it *continue* as a black congregation throughout its history? Was it a *continuous* congregation? In the account cited, it says further, "the first pastor was assigned to Prince George's Circuit in 1868." Does this mean that the first *black* pastor or a *station* pastor? There are a number of research questions to be answered and documents to be found.

[4] Words used by William B. McClain in an address at the Harry Hoosier Banquet, Philadelphia, Pa., May 17, 1980. This is an annual event held by the Black United Methodist Churches in Philadelphia.

[5] Joshua E. Licorish, *Harry Hoosier, African Pioneer Preacher* (Philadelphia: Afro-Methodist Associates, 1967).

and keenness."[6] There exists a line drawing of Hoosier's kindly face, with special attention to the eyes described. Virginia J. Kiah of Savannah, Georgia, has painted an oil portrait which now hangs in St. George's United Methodist Church in Philadelphia.

Although he could neither read nor write, "he had a quick mind, a most retentive memory, and such an eloquent flow of words, which he could soon put into almost faultless English." G. A. Raybold wrote in 1849:

> Harry could remember passages of Scripture and quote them accurately; and hymns, also, which he had heard read, he could repeat or sing. He was never at a loss in preaching, but he was very acceptable wherever he went, and few of the white preachers could equal him, *in his way*.[7]

Obviously, Raybold's qualification of "in his way" refers to that resplendent tradition of black preaching of which Harry was a pioneer and master. He commends further as to his "Preaching abilities, complete command of his voice, aptness in language, and free delivery, as to Scripture and doctrinal truth."[8]

Dr. Benjamin Rush, noted physician of Philadelphia, signer of the Declaration of Independence, abolitionist, and later friend to the Bethelites heard Hoosier and remarked: "Making allowances for his illiteracy, he was the greatest orator in America.[9]

Dr. Thomas Coke had Hoosier as a travelling companion on his first preaching tour through Delaware, Maryland and Virginia—a distance of about one thousand miles. Coke records in his *Journal* that "He (Asbury) has given me his black Harry and borrowed an excellent horse from me." But it was not until Coke heard Hoosier preach that he made an assess-

---

[6] See Warren Thomas Smith, *Harry Hoosier: Circuit Rider* (Nashville: The Upper Room, 1981), p. 18.

[7] Quoted in *ibid.*, p. 24; italics added.

[8] Stevens, II, p. 174f.

[9] *Ibid.*, p. 176.

ment of Hoosier's preaching. Obviously "Black Harry" won his heart. After hearing him *several times* he recorded, on November 29, 1784:

> I have now had the pleasure of hearing Harry preach several times. I sometimes give notice immediately after preaching, that in a little time Harry will preach to the blacks; but the whites always stay to hear him. Sometimes I publish him to preach at candle-light, as the Negroes can better attend at that time.[9]

Bishop Coke then goes on to give his assessment of Harry's ability to preach:

> I really believe that he is one of the best preachers in the world—there is such an amazing power as attends his word, though he cannot read, and he is one of the humblest creatures I ever saw.[10]

In 1786 Hoosier accompanied Asbury to New York and preached for the first time at John Street Church in the early autumn. *The New York Packet* gave a detailed write-up of this event:

> Lately came to this city a very singular black man, who, it is said, is quite ignorant of letters, yet he has preached in the Methodist Church several times to the acceptance of several well-disposed, judicious people. He delivers his discourses with great zeal and pathos, and his language and connection is by no means contemptible. It is the wish of several of our correspondents that this same black man may be so successful as to rouse the dormant zeal of members of our slothful white people, who seem very little affected about concerns of another world.[11]

During 1786–1788, Hoosier travelled with Richard Whatcoat, the Presiding Elder of Delaware, Eastern Maryland and Eastern Pennsylvania. Whatcoat reports that in 1778 no fewer than 847 black members were added to the membership rolls. We cannot know how much Hoosier's eloquent preaching accounts for that number; many probably first at-

[10] *Ibid.*
[11] September 11, 1786.

tended because of Harry's reputed ability to preach so persuasively and effectively. Years after the two had preached
at Dock Creek, Maryland, their sermons were "long remembered."[12]

It was Freeborn Garrettson who introduced Harry Hoosier
to New England. He records the response of the people as
enthusiastic: the "people of this circuit were amazingly fond
of hearing Harry." The preaching tour was not without its
problems as Harry encountered the harsh racist attitudes
present in the society. Garrettson records their encounter at
Hartford: "while Harry gave an exhortation some rude people behaved uncivilly."[13]

It was at Boston that Harry Hoosier met the founder and
the first Grand Master of the first Grand Lodge of Negro
Masons, Prince Hall. Hall had become a Methodist in 1774.
Garrettson arranged for Harry Hoosier to stay at Hall's
home. Garrettson records in his *Journal:* "I boarded Harry
with the Master Mason for the Africans." On this tour he
also met Jesse Lee, the founder of New England Methodism
and preached alongside him in that New England "clime."

Harry Boehm, the son of Bishop Martin Boehm of the
United Brethren in Christ, had a chance to hear Harry
Hoosier at the Philadelphia Conference of 1803. He is almost
ecstatic in his *Reminiscences:* "I heard during the session, a
number of admirable sermons . . . I also heard "Black
Harry," who travelled with Bishop Asbury and Freeborn
Garrettson. He was a perfect character, could neither read
nor write, and yet was very eloquent. His sermon was one of
great eloquence and power." Responding to those who
thought Harry must have been of English blood to be so
eloquent, Boehm gave an instant reply: "Harry was very
black, an African of the Africans." Boehm's assessment of
Hoosier's preaching is almost extreme: "His voice was pure
music and his tongue, as the pen of a ready writer. He was

[12]Smith, *op. cit.,* p. 38.
[13]*Ibid.,* p. 42.

unboundedly popular, and many would rather hear him than the bishops."[14]

It is said by some of his peers that Harry "fell from grace" near the end of his life and became addicted to drink. But Abel Stevens, the Methodist historian, reports:

> "God restored him to the joys of his salvation. Thence-forward he continued faithful. He resumed his public labors, and about the year 1810 (1806, actually) died in Philadelphia 'making a good end,' and was borne to the grave by a great procession of both white and black admirers, who buried him as a hero, once overcome, but finally victorious."[15]

And a hero's burial he deserved. For an illiterate slave to rise to the top of the preaching profession and to be acclaimed by those at the top as being greater than they was no small feat. He was surely a rare human being who used his gifts and graces to ride the circuit of early Methodism as a son of thunder, declaring the good news of Jesus Christ to *all* who would hear him. He was a horseman for the Lord and left a legacy that is bequeathed to all who follow in this line of splendor. The chapter of his life is one of those unheralded epics of the early black Methodists struggling to make sense of being black and Methodist. He made an inestimable contribution to the history of Methodism.

JOHN STEWART: MISSIONARY TO WYANDOTTE INDIANS

The home missions enterprise in the Methodist Church was inspired and perhaps received its birth from John Stewart, a black preacher of Methodism. Reporting on the General Conference of 1820, Frederick Norwood recorded the establishment of a special agency for home missions:

> Stimulated by the highly original activity of black lay preacher John Stewart who worked among the Wyandot Indians of Ohio, the general conference gave its blessing to the infant

---

[14] *Ibid.*, p. 49.
[15] Stevens, *op. cit.*, p. 175.

organization in its purpose to spread scriptural holiness by means of a special agency. For the first time, the Methodist Episcopal Church made a distinction between itself, understood totally as a missionary movement ("to spread scriptural holiness") and a special department whose responsibility was mission.[16]

In 1919 American Methodism celebrated its Century Movement of missions reporting on that successful celebration that $140,000,000 was raised for foreign and home missions. Dr. Edgar Blake reported to the 1920 Northern General Conference: "I am bound to say this, that in the light of the whole situation, the success of the Centenary financial campaign is the most remarkable and striking financial achievement in the history of America, if not in the history of the world."[17] Historians have credited John Stewart's work as the moving force behind the celebration: "Launched to commemorate the beginning of Methodist missions among the Wyandotte Indians by John Stewart, the illiterate Negro preacher in 1819, the Centenary captured the imagination of the Christian world."[18]

John Stewart was born in Powhatan County, Virginia, around 1786. He was a freeborn mulatto.[19] By age 21, he had decided to see other parts of the settled United States and set out for Ohio. But early in his travels he was robbed of all he possessed. This experience caused Stewart to do some serious thinking about himself and his future. Although his parents were practicing Baptists, John was described as a "careless sinner."[20]

He became addicted to drugs and alcohol, but a nagging conscience continued to haunt him. Perhaps the loss of his

---

[16]Frederick A. Norwood, *The Story of American Methodism* (Nashville: Abingdon Press, 1974), p. 177.

[17]The Daily Christian Advocate, May 7, 1920, p. 117.

[18]*The History of American Methodism*, edited by Emory Stevens Bucke (Nashville: Abingdon Press, 1964), p. 400.

[19]Joseph Mitchell, *The Missionary Pioneer, John Stewart, Man of Color* (New York: J. Emory and B. Waugh, 1827), p. 14.

[20]Graham, p. 6.

possessions, the distance from home, the state of poverty and disgrace all compounded to bring him to the brink of despair. He contemplated suicide on several occasions. One night, on the way to the river to drown himself, he was attracted by hymn singing in the distance. As he drew nearer, it became more appealing. When he arrived at the site from which the sound was coming, he discovered it was a Methodist prayer meeting.

Now Stewart had been raised in a strict Baptist home and had been taught prejudice against the Methodists. This is not surprising as black people of the rural South were deprived of any real organized social existence. Outside of the family, the church represented their widest social orientation. And, being outsiders to the American community, it was the church which enlisted their deepest loyalties. Such loyalties were often expressed in fierce and fanatical denominationalism, often fostered by the white missionaries and preachers from whom they first heard the Gospel.

E. Franklin Frazier reported a related incident in rural Alabama. A black person, when asked to identify the people in the adjoining community replied, "The nationality in there is Methodist." Frazier added the comments, "For the Negro masses, in their social and moral isolation in American society, the Negro church community has been a nation within a nation."[21]

In any case, Stewart's curiosity, and perhaps his own agony of soul, won out over his denominational proclivities, and he entered the meeting to discover a cordial reception from the Methodists. He was encouraged by them to seek with all his heart the "last blessing." He found himself at one with them.

Later, he attended a camp meeting conducted by the Reverend Marcus Lindsey, a Methodist preacher from the Marietta Circuit; this is where John Stewart was converted, near day-break from the "mourner's bench" to a lively Chris-

---

[21] E. Franklin Frazier, *The Negro Church in America* (New York: Schocken Books, 1974), p. 49.

tian faith. The conversion issued forth into a regular devotional life. At one such time during his evening devotion he felt called to preach, but resisted the call, mainly because he felt himself unworthy. While bed-ridden during a serious illness, he made the promise to preach. When he recovered he kept it.

John Graham described his journey: "Without bread or credential, he crossed the Muskingum River" and found "friendly enemies on the other side of the river."[22] They introduced him to the tribe of Delawares on the upper Sandusky River. It was here that Stewart started his ministry.

The first congregation he preached to had a grand total of two: an old Indian man named Big Tree and an aged Wyandotte woman named Mary. Perhaps they were among the few who understood English. To overcome the language problem, Stewart sought the help of a subaltern among the Indians, William Walker, one who befriended him and encouraged him to continue his ministry then and many times later. Walker directed him to Jonathan Pointer, a black man who had been taken prisoner by the tribe in his youth. Pointer had learned to speak the language of his captors rather fluently. Stewart did not find Pointer enthusiastic either about his mission or his message; others had made futile attempts before him. Upon learning that Pointer was preparing to attend a tribal feast and dance, Stewart asked to accompany him. With some persuasion, Pointer reluctantly consented.

Stewart was determined to preach the gospel that had saved him from despair and felt that he had a chance at the festival where the tribe had assembled. He asked permission to speak to the gathering. At the end of his message, he requested those who entertained feelings of friendship and good will to indicate by extending to him their right hand. The tribal chief—Two Logs—gave immediate response. He rose and informed the group that they were obligated to

[22]John Graham, p. 7.

show friendship to this stranger who had come into their midst. Taking the lead, he extended his right hand and his tribesmen followed. Still determined to declare the "unsearchable riches of the Kingdom," Stewart announced that he would preach at Pointer's house and invited all to attend.[23]

The Wyandotte Indian tribe responded to the gospel that Stewart preached; first, Big Tree and later other tribal leaders: Monocue, Between-the-Log, Peacock and others. Between-the-Log and Monocue became local preachers. By 1822 Bishop William McKendree visited the mission and found it had a membership of 200.

John Stewart was without credentials, which the white traders in the territory used in order to accuse Stewart of being a runaway slave. Again Walker defended his ministry and encouraged Stewart to continue his work. The Roman Catholic missionaries accused Stewart of preaching a doctrine antithetical to the teachings of the Church. A trial was held with Walker as judge, the ruling was that Stewart's Bible was in English and the Catholic version in Latin. Again Stewart was sustained.

In March of 1819, two months before the first home missions agency was established, Stewart was given credentials. At a quarterly meeting of the Mud River Circuit at Urbana, Ohio, several of the Wyandotte converts accompanied Stewart to recommend that he be granted a local preacher's license. Moses Crane, the presiding elder of the Miami District, licensed him at that conference.

Stewart's biographer indicates that at high noon on September 17, 1823 he passed from his mission with the Wyandotte Indians to the portals of glory. After calling his wife to his bedside and articulating faintly the words: "Wife, be faithful," he breathed his last at age 37.[24] He was buried in the center of the Indian reservation on the Upper Sandusky

[23]See Mitchell, pp. 30 ff.; also W. W. Sweet, *Methodism in American History* (New York: Methodist Book Concern, 1933), pp. 190ff.

[24]*Ibid.*, p. 93.

where he had labored and from which he passed to reward.

This black son of thunder used his gifts and graces to extend the gospel and Methodism to his red brothers and sisters. He opened the way for Methodism to take more seriously its mission to those natives of American soil about whom Methodism, up to this point, had been indifferent.[25] He was the pioneer of home missions.

HENRY EVANS: CHURCH ORGANIZER

Another of the Boanerges, "who feared not the face of man"[26] was Henry Evans, a giant among the early Methodist preachers. Unlike Harry Hoosier who preached primarily in the North and travelled from place to place to meet new congregations and crowds day after day, Evans was an organizer and a pastor to both whites and blacks. Bishop William Capers notes that "he was confessedly the father of the Methodist Church, white and black, in Fayetteville, and the best preacher of his time in that quarter."[27]

Henry Evans was born in Virginia, a free black man and shoemaker by trade. While a young man he was converted

[25] Even though John Wesley's stated reason for coming to Georgia was "to learn the true sense of the gospel of Christ by preaching to the heathen," and "to convert the Indian," (*Letters*, I, p. 187) a rather selfish and naive reason. His naive faith and cultural arrogance led him to conclude that the native's "great expectation of a white man to teach them wisdom" was confirmed when the Indians met him and offered him gifts of milk and honey in witness of their longing that he would nourish them in strength and deal with them monthly (*Journal*, February 14, 1736). However, his opinions of the American Indians changed dramatically: he decided that they were poor subjects for the gospel, "all, except perhaps the Choctaws, gluttons, drunkards, thieves, dissemblers, liars." (*Journal*, February 8 and 14, 1737). Indeed, he confessed that they were "implacable, unmerciful; murderers of fathers, murderers of mothers, murders of their own children" and unspeakably promiscuous of sexual offense. It is an irony of history that John Stewart, a black preacher, became the first effective Methodist missionary to the Indians 80 years later.

[26] William Capers, a white zealous worker in the evangelization of the slaves, successor to Evans at Fayetteville and later bishop in the southern Methodist Church, provided much biographical information on Evans in his autobiography. This is one of the expressions used by Capers about Evans printed in William M. Wightman, *William Capers, Including an Autobiography* (Nashville: Southern Methodist Publishing House, 1858), p. 126.

[27] *Ibid.*, p. 124.

to Christianity and became an itinerant local preacher in the Methodist Church. John W. Coleman, a former pastor in Wilmington, Delaware, credits him with organizing the Fourth Street Church in that city.[28]

A short time after, he decided to move to Charleston, South Carolina, thinking he might better succeed at his trade. En route to Charleston, Evans stopped at Fayetteville, North Carolina. While there he attended services at Duggs Chapel and introduced himself as a Methodist local preacher. There being no preacher of any denomination for the slaves in that town, he accepted the invitation of some of the white citizens to preach to the slaves. Capers related the story in detail. He began to "preach to the Negroes with great effect." Soon his preaching was considered threatening to the social situation and the town council barred him from further preaching. Nothing in his considerable persuasive power could prevail upon them to permit him to preach. He then withdrew to the sand hills outside of the city limits and held meetings in the woods, "changing his appointments from place to place." Since he was violating no law, "the council was effectually eluded," but not the mob. Opposition grew, but he continued to preach in different locations. His labor bore fruit in the lives of his hearers and word spread from the slaves to their owners about the power and sincerity of Evans' preaching.

Capers reports that the whites decided that they too should hear him as there was not a single church and but one congregation (Presbyterian) in the town: "Now, too, of the mistresses there were not a few, and some masters, who were brought to think that the preaching which had proved so beneficial to their servants might be good for them also; and the famous Negro preacher had some whites as well as blacks to hear him."[29]

On the power of Evans' preaching, there was "a change in the current of opinion" and the action of the town council was rescinded, allowing Evans again to preach in Fayette-

[28] Coleman, p. 7.
[29] *Ibid.*

ville. Soon a meeting house was built which was described as "a frame of wood, weatherboarded only on the outside, without plastering, about fifty feet long by thirty feet wide."[30]

Joseph Travis, the presiding elder of the Pee Wee District of the South Carolina Conference, described the development of what later became Evans Chapel Church:

> He began more and more to elicit the attention of the white population. Ultimately, a white married lady of good mind and accomplished manners—a celebrated school mistress—joined the Methodist Episcopal Church . . . prejudice . . . began to melt like wax before the flame. Other white citizens presented themselves for admission. His congregation became larger and respectable . . . he . . . transferred church, congregation and all over to the white preachers.[31]

Capers indicates that the whites crowded out the black members. "And now there was no longer room for the Negroes in the house when Evans preached." The weatherboards were knocked out and "sheds were added to the house on either side" to accommodate the crowds.

In 1810 Evans appeared from the little shed that was adjacent to the chancel, which was his humble dwelling, for his final time. Capers, who was then the pastor, described it in reverent detail:

> The little door between his humble shed and the chancel where I stood was opened and the dying man entered for a last farewell to his people. He was almost too feeble to stand at all, but supporting himself by the railing of the chancel, he said: 'I have come to say my last word to you. It is this: None but Christ. Three times I have had my life in jeopardy for preaching the gospel to you. Three times I have broken the ice on the edge of the water and swam across the Cape Fear to preach the gospel to you. And now, if in my last hour I could trust to that or to any thing else but to Christ crucified, for my salvation, all should be lost and my soul perish forever.'[32]

[30] *Ibid.*

[31] Joseph Travis, *Autobiography of the Rev. Joseph Travis*, p. 101f. Quoted in Graham, *op. cit.*, *p. 4.*

[32] Wightman, p. 129.

He was buried under the chancel of the church which he had founded and which bore his name. But Evans left an indelible impression on the City of Fayetteville and on the history of the Methodist Church. He had preached to whites and blacks where it was socially disapproved and later forbidden. There is no evidence anywhere that he compromised the gospel. Perhaps there is a great deal of poetry, and yet certainly the spirit of the man and his work in Gayraud Wilmore's statement: "When the lash was cutting the backs of men like Evans, the thought was burned into their flesh with every blow, that for all their protestations, the slaveholding Christians knew that their system was doomed because it was abhorrent to the God they professed to serve."[33]

The shame and guilt that made the mob want to silence Evans did not prevail. Even with his life in jeopardy three times for preaching the gospel, this son of thunder could not be silenced. Nor would he compromise his dignity by surrendering to a false and faulty definition of who a man was. He would not accommodate himself to the misguided expectations of the majority. The inclusivity of his local church, with him at the helm, was both a witness to the gospel and its insistence on the nature of the Kingdom, and an indictment of a church which would soon compromise its principles and transform the absolute and ideal ethics of the Lord into a relativistic and pragmatic accommodation.

---

[33] *Wilmore, p. 108.*

VI

METHODISM AND SLAVERY:
A Tragic Moral Reversal

THE FATEFUL EXCEPTION

As previously noted, from the very beginning John Wesley was inalterably opposed to slavery and the slave trade which he described as "that execrable sum of all villainies."[1] Wesley asked: "Did the Creator intend that the noblest creations in the visible world should live such a life as this?" The last book that octogenarian Wesley read was *The Interesting Narrative of the Life of Olandah Equiano.* The testimony of this black West Indian stimulated him to write his final letter to William Wilberforce, encouraging him to keep up the fight against slavery, a letter which was cited earlier.

The first official action taken against slavery in American Methodism by the Baltimore Conference of Methodist Societies in 1780 reflected these views of Wesley. In that conference, meeting under the supervision of Asbury, there was included *Question Seventeen* which asked: *Does this conference acknowledge that slavery is contrary to the law of God, man and nature and hurtful to society?*

The assembly answered with a "Yes!" The conference then went on record recognizing its duty to do something about slavery. The influence of Wesley had leaped across the Atlantic and the vile institution of slavery came to be perceived as being a moral matter which had to be dealt with by actions

---

[1] *Wesley, Journal,* V. p. 445

leading to its elimination, and an evil which could not be condoned or tolerated within the Methodist movement.

The conference meeting in Baltimore that spring evidenced its determination that any eliminating action should begin with the travelling preachers; thus, Question Sixteen was asked of the conference members. That group included forty-two slave-holding preachers. That question was: *Ought not this conference require those travelling preachers who hold slaves to give promise to set them free?* The answer again was "Yes!" The die was cast. The position had been taken. The time for action had come!

Unfortunately, as we shall see, the action taken was not the unequivocal act of suspension of slave-holding preachers, but instead a rush to discover a way of compromise rather than to impose the strict penalty of suspension. The door to compromise on this moral issue was opened and has never been securely and permanently closed from that day to this.

In 1784, the Methodist Church came into being at the now-famous Christmas Conference at Lovely Lane Chapel, Baltimore. On that crisp winter morning at 10 o'clock when the Conference was called into session, sixty of the eighty-one ministers who had been found by Garrettson during his six-week ride were present. Also present at that historic session where the Methodist Episcopal Church was born were "Black Harry" Hoosier and Richard Allen, who was later to father the African Methodist Episcopal Church. From the very beginning of the official Methodist Episcopal Church, black people were an integral part.

After reading Wesley's letter of instructions, adopting it as their agenda, dealing with ministerial relations, and approving the content of what was to become a *Book of Discipline*, the Conference members arrived at *Question Forty-two* of the items before them: *"What methods can we take to extirpate slavery?"* The answer:

> We are deeply conscious of the impropriety of making new terms of communion for a religious society already estab-

lished, excepting on the most pressing occasion: and such we esteem the practice of holding our fellow creatures in slavery. We view it as contrary to the Golden Law of God on which hang all the Laws and the Prophets and the inalienable rights of mankind, as well as every principle of the revolution to hold in the deepest abasement in a more abject slavery than is perhaps to be found in any part of the world except America, so many souls that are capable of the Image of God.

We therefore think that our bounded duty to take immediately some effectual method to extirpate this abomination from among us.[2]

The answer was a clear and ringing denunciation of slavery, and the rule adopted was one that was sweeping in its intention to be applied to preachers and lay people alike. All Methodists were required to embark upon a procedure whereby any slaves they held would be emancipated. Those who refused were to be excluded from the church. And, no new persons who held slaves were to be admitted to membership in the church.

This far-reaching and sweeping antislavery position taken by the Methodists was greeted with glee by the slaves who got the news. The novelist Alex Haley accurately reconstructs the early social history of his own denomination in his book, *Roots,* when he "factions" and puts these words into the mouth of a slave:

> Methodists (done) called a great big meetin' in Baltimore an' finally dey 'greed slavin' was 'gainst Gawd's laws an' dat anybody callin' hisself Christian wouldn't have it did to deyselves, so it's mostly de Methodists an' Quakers makin' church fuss to git laws to free niggers.[3]

But, unfortunately, time, events, clumsiness, and compromise revealed the action they took to be little more than just that, "church fuss," at least for a time. Although there were many courageous preachers who fought in support of the Christmas Conference's position in opposition to slavery

[2]M. W. Simpson, *Encyclopedia of Methodism* (Philadelphia: Everts and Everts, 1878), p. 805.

[3]Alex Haley, *Roots* (Garden City, N.Y.: Doubleday, 1976), p. 353.

and joined forces with anti-slavery groups; so successful
were those who opposed the Conference's stand that later
Jesse Lee, one of the leading Methodist abolitionists, could
write:

> These rules (against slavery) were short-lived, and were of-
> fensive to most of our southern friends; and were so much
> opposed by many . . . that the execution of them was sus-
> pended at the conference held in June following . . . and they
> were never afterwards carried into full force . . . (at) the Gen-
> eral Conference in 1808 . . . the greater part of the rule . . . Was
> abolished, and no part of it was retained respecting private
> members.[4]

Asbury and Coke fought vigorously and courageously,
but to no avail. At the conference which met at Baltimore on
June 1, 1785, six months later, they, too, conceded. The rules
established at the Christmas Conference were to be applied
only as far as they were *consistent* with the laws of the states
in which the members resided. This fateful exception referred to the laws forbidding emancipation already enacted
in some of the southern states. Now, antislavery legislation
was suspended altogether and never reappeared in that
form. Moral compromise, the devouring demon of truth,
and right, and discipleship, had won the day and would
characterize the resolutions, decisions, and practices of the
Church for a long time.

Compromises which had once tortured the conscience became virtuous in themselves. It was probably at this point
that the Methodist Church became most accommodating to a
developing American way of life. Methodism and its way of
dealing with the question of the presence of black people
became virtually parallel to the story of American morality.
Although there are reflected in both the church and the nation, economic, political, social and psychological beliefs,
these are not framed in moral terms.

Faced with the dilemma of choosing between the laws of

---

[4]See Leroy M. Lee, *The Life and Times of the Rev. Jesse Lee* (Louisville: John Early for
the M.E. Church South, 1848). Quoted in Coleman, pp. 19–20.

God and the laws of man, the Methodist Church felt it was not the province of the church to contravene the established legal provisions of the civil authority; and yielded obedience to the laws of man, "rendering unto Caesar" the things that rightly belonged to God. Truly the study of the Methodist Church and its dealings with its black constituency is a study of American morality. And the drama still unfolds.

ECONOMIC AND RELIGIOUS RATIONALE FOR ALLOWING SLAVERY

Subsequently, an event occurred which made the plight of enslaved black people even more serious and their chance for freedom more hopeless. In 1793, Eli Whitney invented the cotton gin. The economically beneficial results of this invention produced an attitudinal change regarding slavery both in the North and the South. Cotton began to dominate the markets of the world with such economic impact that the dizzying demand for the product ushered the question of morality regarding slavery right out of the window in many quarters.

With the European demand for raw cotton, coupled with the demand of the new cotton mills of the North, not enough cotton could be raised to satisfy the cry for greater and greater quantities of the product. But the actual raising of cotton was still a matter of hand labor; thus, the demand for more and more slaves increased considerably.

Many Northerners were indirectly involved in the cotton economy which undergirded and increased slavery. Cotton was grown in the South but the manufacture of cotton products was in the North. This produced a growing tolerance toward slavery in the final half of the nineteenth century. In addition, the large numbers of white immigrants to America from Europe became competitors for the unskilled jobs which would otherwise have gone to blacks. These factors coupled together produced a church with a rather docile position on the question of slavery. It retreated from its earlier position. It must be added that the leadership of the church was more concerned about unity and growth of membership than the evils of slavery. As H. V. Richardson put it: "The Church was more interested in growth than in a moral crusade."[5]

The southern churchmen resorted to any and every apologia imaginable to provide a defense and a rationalization for the support of the evil of slavery. Of all the grandiosely hypocritical tactics and rationalizations offered by churchmen in support of slavery, none was so repugnant and damnable as their appeal to, and use of, the Holy Scripture to provide justification for the brutal enslavement of one human being by another. The Apostle Paul is still, at this writing, trying to crawl out from under a "cloud of disdain" because of the repeated use of passages from a few of his letters which purported to support slavery. The southern apologists for slavery sought to convince themselves and others that "He who fights against slavery, then fights against God. For God saw that slavery would be a blessing to both master and slave."

The missionaries to the slaves began to hold the slave-masters guiltless. Slaveholders were not only seen as guiltless because society and economic factors gave them no choice but to be slaveholders, they were also seen as guiltless because a master-slave relationship was simply not a breach of morality. Thus, when Thomas E. Bond, the editor of the *Christian Advocate and Journal*, began to define slavery as a moral evil, the southern churchmen were incensed. They demanded that he be removed from office. It was bad enough to have discussed slavery, they believed, but it was even worse to have called it a moral evil.[6]

It was William Wightman, editor of the *Southern Christian Advocate*, Bond's southern counterpart, who developed a theory of relations between Church and state. The Methodists had not until this time adhered to any strict theory of

[5] Richardson, p. 58.
[6] See Matthews, pp. 236ff.

separation between secular and sacred worlds. They preached in the state legislatures (several as chaplains to the House and Senate), passed petitions regarding Indian trade, and regularly sent memorials regarding temperance to the state assemblies. Countering Bond, Wightman maintained that Methodism was not opposed to slavery in any way. If it were, then it would be opposed to the state and therefore in a revolutionary position impossible for Christians. Thus, Wightman maintained that southern ministers who valued their mission to the slaves would leave the Church should it ever depart from his doctrine of "noninterference with the 'rights of Caesar.'" Subsequent developments were to show that even though Wightman was simply stating his own ideas, he spoke for the southern church.

THE SCHISM OVER SLAVERY

But while the majority of southern churchmen were working overtime sacrificing the truth of the Gospel to that unrelenting goddess "economic profit at-any-cost," even as they knew the argument that God had ordained slavery was a lie, there were those courageous churchmen who would not let justice sleep, nor have truth and right rendered totally impotent by those who would sanction condoning evil for the sake of unity in the church. At first their numbers were small and their cries little more than futile shouts in the face of an overwhelming storm. But there were some sensitive ears who heard their shouts as the "still small voice of God," and came forth to join them in the fight against "the horrid crime" against humanity. Their numbers grew and the antislavery movement within the church gained momentum.

This new wave of abolitionism intensified. From 1836 until 1840 almost every annual conference outside of the south was besieged with petitions calling for the end of slavery. Although the bishops struggled to keep the lid on and prevent the abolitionists from fomenting disruption that threatened to split the church, they did not succeed. At the

General Conference of 1844, the inevitable happened. The denomination that had been born sixty years before in Baltimore became two separate denominations, one South and one North, over the issue of slavery, and remained divided for almost a century. The price of reunion was costly to the blacks who remained in the Methodist Episcopal Church.

The price eventually paid by the nation to eliminate slavery was the bloody, costly Civil War in which more than 600,000 lives were lost. And, as the Northern Army of the Union advanced into the South shouting the battle cry of freedom, following close at hand were the stalwart Methodist soldiers in the Army of the Lord extending the arm of mercy, compassion, love, and material help to the newly freed slaves.

One of the results of the schism of the church was the development of a renewed and more passionate interest on the part of the Southern Church in evangelizing the slaves. William Capers was one of the most zealous workers in this effort. It is said of him, "He developed a type of organization for serving the slaves which swept over the entire South."[7] And indeed he did. By 1860 there were 171,857 black members. This vigorous evangelization program continued until the Civil War. At the end of the war and with emancipation, these black members were set up as an independent denomination, having fraternal relations with the Southern Church, and receiving financial aid from the benevolence of the white church. And thus another black *Methodist* church, the Colored Methodist Episcopal Church (now the Christian Methodist Episcopal Church) was born.

The schism did not have the same effect immediately upon the North. As Willis J. King pointed out: "Despite their espousal of the freedom of the slaves, local attitudes against the admission of Negroes into the churches changed slowly; and in a number of cases Negroes were encouraged to set up

[7] Willis J. King, "The Central Jurisdiction" in Bucke, ed., *The History of Methodism*, p. 486.
[8] *Ibid.*, pp. 486–487.

their own local congregations or to join the independent Negro denominations."[8] The total number of blacks reported in 1850 was 26,309. The Civil War, however, produced an increased interest in the work of the Northern Church with black people.

VII
POST WAR METHODISM:
Two Evangelization Plans for Blacks

When the General Conference of 1864 met in Philadelphia on May 2, the victory of the Union Army seemed imminent and the end of the war was in view. High on the agenda of that conference was the development of a plan for the evangelization of the newly-freed blacks in the South. The plan called for two avenues of approach: 1) to establish separate black missionary annual conferences in the overall structure of the Methodist Episcopal Church; and 2) to invade the South with teachers and missionaries to aid the blacks in adjusting to their new status as citizens. The plan developed was a tentative answer to the church's question: "What shall we do with the blacks?"

The first black missionary conference to be established was the Delaware Conference which convened its first session at what is now Tindley Temple Church in Philadelphia, Pennsylvania, in 1864. It included black Methodists from the state of Delaware and eastern Maryland and churches in New Jersey and Philadelphia. Bishop Matthew Simpson stated the rationale for establishing these conferences:

1. "colored people preferred to meet in distinct congregations and separate conferences for they felt that they were not treated as equal in mixed congregations or conferences;
2. the desire for mixed intimate association with each other in all church arrangements.

In addition, this fellowship would provide for the Negroes

the only technique to develop within themselves a sense of worth."[1]

In the fall of the same year the second mission conference to be established for blacks was the Washington Conference, which was organized at Sharp Street Church in Baltimore, Maryland. It included black churches in Maryland, the District of Columbia, West Virginia and parts of western Pennsylvania and Virginia.

In 1869, the Lexington Conference was organized at Harrodsburg, Kentucky. It was later to include churches in Ohio, Illinois, Indiana, Michigan, Wisconsin, and Minnesota as well as those churches located in Kentucky.

Other mission conferences were organized in the succeeding years; generally along the state lines to include Florida, Mississippi, Georgia, Alabama, Texas, Tennessee, Arkansas, Missouri and so on throughout the South. In some cases the states were divided to include two conferences. These conferences were served by white bishops and in some cases there were white ministers on loan from the white conferences of the Northern Church for a period of time. But the bulk of the preachers were black—some totally illiterate, but soon to be introduced to education by the work of the Freedman's Aid Society and the Woman's Home Missionary Society.

In the 1864 General Conference the vote was taken to deny the mission conferences the right to send delegates to the quadrennial national meeting. But two of the eight conferences that existed in 1868, the Delaware and the Washington Conferences, elected delegates to attend the General Conference. They were James Davis of the Delaware Conference and Benjamin Brown from the Washington Conference. The General Conference debated the issue for ten days and finally voted to rescind its 1864 action. This vote granted the status to the mission conferences of Annual Conferences, thereby granting the first blacks in the history of the Church

---

[1]Quoted in Graham, p. 36.

the right to be seated in the lawmaking body of Methodism.

These Annual Conferences were to exist as segregated units in the Methodist Church for more than a century. The last conference, the South Carolina Conference, was merged with the white Annual Conference in 1972. But these black structures functioned as the organizational units to which black local churches related for a century. They were black conferences for black churches; and black churches were for black people. As Robert E. Jones, later to be elected the first black bishop of the Methodist Church, described it in 1916: "To all intents and purposes the Negro is as separated as anyone should desire. He has his separated churches, his separated Conferences and the only points of contact are on the general committees at the General Conference."[2]

The second part of the evangelization plan for the ex-slaves was the establishment of schools and colleges for training leaders for citizenship in a democratic nation, and for special leadership in the work of the church. The Freedmen's Aid Society was established in Cincinnati, Ohio, in 1866 to work for "the relief and education of the Freedmen and people of color in general to cooperate with the Missionary and Church Extension Societies of the Methodist Episcopal Church."[3] The first appeal for its support indicates its philosophy:

> The emancipation of four million of slaves has opened at our very door a wide field calling alike for mission and educational work. It has developed upon the Church a fearful responsibility. Religion and education alone can make freedom a blessing to them. *The school must be planted by the side of the church;* the teacher must go along with the missionary . . . from among themselves the ministers are to be raised up who shall conserve, carry forward, and make permanent the work of Christianizing and educating the race.[4]

[2] Dwight Culver, *Negro Segregation in the Methodist Church* (New Haven: Yale University Press, 1953), p. 82.

[3] *Official Report of the Organization Convention of the Freedmen's Aid Society*, p. 10. Quoted by Willis J. King in Bucke, ed., *History of Methodism*, p. 487.

[4] James P. Brawley, *Two Centuries of Methodist Concern: Bondage, Freedom and Education of Black People* (New York: Vantage Press, 1974), p. 61. Italics added.

Within the first seventeen months of the operation of the Society, fifty-nine schools were established in ten states in the South. The early schools established were of necessity elementary schools. But in 1868 there were three normal schools and institutes. Some of the elementary schools developed into academies and preparatory schools within a few years and later into colleges. After 1872 less emphasis was placed upon the establishment of elementary schools and more emphasis upon the development of schools already established.

These schools provided professional preparation in theology, teacher training, medicine, dentistry, and law. Many of the early schools established developed into colleges and universities with courses for preparation in these professional areas. To be sure, at first, to call them "colleges" and "universities" was more of a dream than reality; a hope rather than a fact. But, in time, these hopes were translated into facts. Many of these schools exist today as fine educational institutions that prepare black young people for professional service and careers.[5] Not only do they stand as monuments to the efforts of those who toiled to establish them, often against great odds and with much personal sacrifice; but they also reflect the possibilities, capacities, and abilities of black people to excel when given the opportunity.

THE TWELVE BLACK COLLEGES:
A SPECIAL MINISTRY

The story of the founding of the twelve black colleges traditionally associated with the United Methodist Church is a story of sacrifice, courage, love, heroism, and hope. Founded at a time when the doors of most institutions of higher learning were closed to the recently freed slaves, and when the prevailing attitude of this nation was that black people did not need and were not capable of the de-

[5] *Ibid.*, pp. 81–100.

velopment of their minds, these institutions withstood the pressures and the sentiment against them to become vital centers of education and nurturing. "The school must be planted by the side of the church," stated the original appeal.

And so it was from the beginning of these colleges, a clear understanding that they were to be institutions closely associated with the church to provide culture for service, grounds for socialization, symbols of hope, and the embodiment of the gathered black aspirations.

Many of these colleges, starting in the basements of black churches (as in the case of Bennett College) or in rented houses on the site of a garbage dump (as in the case of Bethune-Cookman College), have become the fulfillment of the dreams of visionary Christians and courageous and committed church people.

The socio-economic conditions of the times shaped the life of these institutions. The deprivation, needs, and hopes, plus the unlimited potential of humans who had been treated as chattel dictated the wide-reaching curriculum; and the commitment of teachers and clergy to strive for excellence in teaching against insuperable odds formed the first chapters of the history of the black colleges of the Methodist Church.

Beginning with Rust College in Mississippi in 1866, these colleges performed veritable miracles with limited financial resources as the veil of ignorance was lifted from a deprived, oppressed, maligned, and dehumanized people. Developing new pedagogies and adjusting the curriculum to cover everything from basic reading to Greek, Latin, geography and higher mathematics, these institutions started on a road that brings us now to this crucial moment in their development. They had the task of preparing leaders for society and for the church. And they were faithful to their tasks. The present record shows that eighty-five percent of the black leadership of the United Methodist Church today received their first degrees from these twelve schools. Six of the eight active black bishops in 1981 were graduates of these schools.

Meharry Medical College, another bastion of educational excellence, is one of two black medical schools in this nation responsible for fifty percent of all black dentists and medical doctors. Its hospital and medical centers serve a vast number of people and continue to pioneer in sensitive research for healing.

While these colleges have always been identified as black colleges, they have always been *open* to all persons, and their faculties throughout their history have had various racial and ethnic backgrounds.

But there is a special ministry that these colleges perform. They are able to take young black people, often from poor families and poor schools and offer the assistance, concern, remediation, and experience necessary for preparation for professions and additional training.

Some are asking why these black colleges continue in an age of integration? How can the existence of the black colleges be justified? Why are black colleges necessary since the 1954 Supreme Court Decision?

First, the problems of racism and economic oppression which were present in this society when these schools were established and continued throughout the history of their existence are still very much in evidence in our present society. Our society is still bedeviled with a heinous racism whose insidious tentacles reach into every aspect of black life. A combination of hopelessness and frustration erupted into a violent explosion in Miami, Florida in May, 1980. Scores of other cities are caldrons of hopelessness, frustration, bitterness, and cynicism as a result of years of unrelieved oppression, economic exploitation, institutional racism, and neglect that is not so benign.

While there is the illusion that much progress has been made, the facts suggest otherwise. Even education has not proven to be the gateway to the good life that so many envisioned. While a few blacks have made dramatic breakthroughs here and there, the record bears out that overall "the more they gained on whites educationally, the more they seem to fall behind economically."[6] The sad fact is that, at this writing, the unemployment rate among black college graduates is higher than the rate of unemployment of white high school dropouts. What this seems to suggest is that there has been more promise than progress, more illusions of achievement than reality.

So the problems of racism and poverty, deprivation and alienation that were present when these schools were established are still present and suggest a continued need for their ministry.

Secondly, if one asks why the need for the black colleges, then one simply needs to look at the alumni of these institutions and the records they have made in academic and community life which validate the teaching and quality *relationships* of the black colleges. Thousands of black professionals who served their communities and have achieved excellent records in graduate studies and professional schools are graduates of these twelve schools; and have found an inspiration and encouragement in these schools peculiar to the nature of these institutions.

Thirdly, present statistics show that fifty percent of black young people who are attending college are enrolled in predominantly black colleges. This suggests that, in the light of the search for black identity and dignity during the last several years, the black colleges play a unique role that only they can play. Many black students need the guidance, personal concern, special assistance, and atmosphere that is found on the predominantly black college campus. Often students encounter a faculty and staff able to deal with problems peculiar to the black student and the black experience

---

[6] *Time Magazine,* June 16, 1980, p. 20.

and, thus, the retention rates for black students at black colleges are much greater than the rates for black students on white college campuses.

Fourthly, the black college is the custodian of black culture, a culture that is valid and valuable, not only for black Americans, but for the whole of the Christian Church and the nation if this nation and the church are to be truly pluralistic. As one of the black college presidents has observed: "Roman Catholics have their Notre Dame and Holy Cross; Jews have their Brandeis and Yeshiva, and black Methodists have their Clark and Bennett."

Fifthly, black colleges ought to continue to exist because they are good educational institutions. There is a subtle implication that these institutions are inferior because they are black and black-controlled. Such familiar thinking and talk is racist and erroneously based on the ideology of white superiority.

Without question, there are some poor black colleges. But there are also some poor white colleges. The color of the administration and the students does not determine the quality of the institution. If for no other reason, the black colleges need to exist to refute and resist the fallacious propaganda that simply underscores the depth of continued racism in our society.

The list of those schools which remain today is impressive: Bennett College, Greensboro, North Carolina; Bethune-Cookman College, Daytona Beach, Florida; Clark College, Atlanta, Georgia; Claflin College, Orangeburg, South Carolina; Dillard University, New Orleans, Louisiana; Gammon Theological Seminary (at Interdenominational Center), Atlanta, Georgia; Huston-Tillotson College, Austin, Texas; Meharry Medical School, Nashville, Tennessee; Morristown College, Morristown, Tennessee; Paine College, (sponsored by the United Methodist Church and the Christian Methodist Episcopal Church), Augusta, Georgia; Philander-Smith College, Little Rock, Arkansas; Rust College, Holly Springs, Mississippi; and Wiley College, Marshall, Texas.

These black Methodist colleges deserve a salute and support for being some of the finest educational institutions in this nation; agencies which perform an important educational ministry. Time has not diminished their mission. The promise, quality, and value of these institutions are still highly significant. They deserve support because they are vital, viable, and relevant institutions in an age when we know all too well: "A mind is a terrible thing to waste."

VIII

THE ESTABLISHMENT OF THE CENTRAL JURISDICTION:
A Cause to Sit and Weep

THE PLAN FOR UNION: SEED OF SEGREGATION

Dr. James P. Brawley, former President of Clark College and a delegate to the so-called "Uniting Conference of 1939," reports that when the Plan for Union was adopted, reuniting the three major erstwhile separated white bodies of Methodism, "delegates arose, after the voting, to sing "We Are Marching Upward to Zion," the Negro delegates remained seated and some of them wept."[1] They had just witnessed the Methodist Church's latest answer to the question: What shall we do with the blacks in the Methodist Church? They had been present as their fate was decided. The Church had voted to establish the Central Jurisdiction, an obvious "symbol of racial exclusiveness."[2] It was the price for reunification. And, as John Graham points out: "The Negro became the 'sacrificial lamb' on the altar in order that union could be consummated."[3]

In the Plan of Union which brought together the Methodist Episcopal Church, the Methodist Episcopal Church, South, and the Methodist Protestant Church, Methodism in the continental United States was divided into six Jurisdic-

[1] James P. Brawley, "Methodist Church from 1939," *Central Christian Advocate,* October 15, 1967, p. 4.

[2] An expression used by Willis J. King to describe the Plan for an all-black Central Jurisdiction at the 1936 General Conference.

[3] Graham, *op. cit.,* p. 90.

tions. Five of these, the Northeastern, Southeastern, North Central, South Central and Western Jurisdictions were to be constituted geographically. The Central Jurisdiction, the sixth, was to be composed of the nineteen black conferences of the former northern Methodist Episcopal Church plus the black mission conferences and other black missions in the United States. By any definition, it was a racially segregated unit of the Church and the policy was written into the Constitution of The Methodist Church. For the first time in the Methodist Episcopal Church history there was an official policy of segregation. While the plan made provisions for the black membership to have equal jurisdictional participation in the national denomination's General Conference, General Boards, Council of Bishops and so on, and gave to the black membership the right to elect its own leadership and establish its own policies and procedures; the Methodist Church was, by the same token, establishing a policy of dealing with its black membership on the basis of race. They were to be segregated at every connectional level of the church's life below that of its national structure.

The Plan was a long time developing. Attempts made in 1865 immediately after the Civil War found the Southern Church embittered and unwilling. Other attempts were made from 1916 to 1939. The Plan of 1924 received a majority vote of the Southern Methodist Episcopal Church Annual Conferences, but failed to get the constitutional majority required. In 1932 the Methodist Episcopal Church and the Methodist Protestant Church established commissions to begin three-sided negotiations. The Methodist Episcopal Church, South, added its commission in 1934. It was from this basic plan developed by the Joint Commission that reunification was effected.

The crucial problem for the Methodist Protestant Church was accepting the office of bishop, but that was hardly the most critical problem. The paramount problem, one of Herculean proportions, remained: *What to do with the 315,000 black Methodists in the Methodist Episcopal Church* (mostly spread across the nineteen annual conferences reaching from Florida to New Jersey).

Dwight W. Culver, in his book *Negro Segregation in The Methodist Church,* is quite convinced that the "status of the Negro" was the most important problem to be dealt with by the Joint Commission on Unification. He relates a comment by Bishop Earl Cranston that gets right to the heart of the matter: "It was thought that if we could come to an agreement as to the status of the Negro, the other matters will adjust themselves to correspond to that understanding."[4]

The Southern Church Commissioners were virtually unanimous in the opinion that they should be formed into a separate denomination of their own, perhaps uniting with the African Methodist Episcopal Church and the Colored Methodist Episcopal Church and the African Methodist Episcopal Church Zion. The Northern Church Commissioners held that such an independent church could not be established except by the will and acting of the black constituents of the Methodist Episcopal Church. They were unwilling to inaugurate such a movement.

It must be pointed out that, although the Northern Church was unwilling to exclude its black members, it had already put into place a system of separate black churches, schools, and annual conferences which were discussed earlier. *The Central Christian Advocate* which it had established, was a journal by, about, and for black Methodists; and three black bishops—Robert E. Jones, Matthew W. Clair and Alexander P. Shaw[5]—were elected by separate ballot. In effect, it had already created "a church within a church." This will be discussed in detail later. In addition, there was no overwhelming movement in the North and the Methodist Episcopal Church to enlist blacks as members of local churches

[4] Culver, *op. cit.,* p. 61. See his whole discussion of "The Negro Issue in the Methodist Unification," pp. 60–78.

[5] There were four other black bishops elected prior to these three, but they were missionary bishops to Liberia. They were Francis Burns, John W. Roberts, Isiah B. Scott and Alexander P. Camphor.

and pastors of white churches. Quite to the contrary, in many cases blacks were encouraged to set up their own local churches or to join the A.M.E. and A.M.E. Zion Churches in the northern cities. The first black Methodist minister to be appointed to serve a white congregation was the Rev. Simon Peter Montgomery at Old Mystic, Connecticut in September, 1955. It was such a departure from the usual as to warrant feature stories in several of the country's leading news magazines; the story was also carried in the *London Times* and other newspapers in Europe. According to the Rev. Montgomery, visitors from forty states and three foreign countries made their way to Old Mystic "to see this thing that has come to pass."[6]

But whatever may have been the views of the Northern Church and its individual members and congregations, there was a rich history of blacks within this church which could not be denied or overlooked. At least, theoretically, it welcomed all groups into its fellowship regardless of race, color, or origin. And, as Willis J. King puts it: "There was fresh in the memories of all concerned the very vigorous evangelistic and educational program the church had carried forward among the freedmen since the close of the Civil War, and there were thousands of Methodists committed to that program."[7] He further suggests that blacks had a legal claim on their rights by virtue of membership: "There was the legal fact that the Negroes were as definitely a part of the church as was any other group in it, and could not be eliminated from its membership except by their own choice."[8]

In developing the Plan for Union, the Joint Commission sought to devise a proposal which would not offend Southern sensibilities and yet adhere to the North's historic mission to blacks. It was the feeling of the Commission that the Plan did both. It effectively isolated the Southern Church

---

[6] This information is based on an interview with the Rev. Simon Peter Montgomery, February 10, 1982.

[7] King, *op. cit.*, p. 488.

[8] *Ibid.*

from virtually all contact with black Methodists. Satisfying their regional concerns, it allowed them to retain a large measure of control over their affairs.[9]

Although there were some influential whites in the Northern Church who resented the ethical implications of the Central Jurisdiction, such as the popular pastor of Evanston, Ernest Fremont Tittle, and Lewis O. Hartman and others; Bishop McConnell probably spoke for the majority of the Northern Church when he recommended it as the best possible for that time, hoping that it would become the basis for a more nearly Christian relationship in the future.

THE BLACK RESPONSE: A SENSE OF OUTRAGE

But black Methodists were vigorous in their opposition to the Plan and immediate in their response. They saw clearly that a separate Jurisdiction based on race was segregation—pure and simple—and they were opposed to segregation. Not only was it unChristian and immoral, it was no time for the Church that had led the way in reform to retreat and say to the nation that segregation could be defended on any grounds.

Black Methodists were not opposed to Unification; they were against segregation. They were not resisting union; they were against the price. Matthew W. Clair, Jr. indicates that the Washington Conference passed a resolution on the state of the church. In that resolution they thanked God for harmony and expressed the desire and hope for the union of Methodism.[10] As one person put it: "They believed in ecumenicity but they refused to be 'ecumaniacs.'"

Speaking against the Plan, David D. Jones, President of Bennett College, said: ". . . Everyone knows the plan is

[9]There was vigorous opposition to the Plan by some Southern churchmen such as Bishop Candler and Collins Denny. Bishop Candler resigned himself to it, commenting: "I'll be in heaven before Unification gets to working good." (Quoted in Norwood, op. cit., p. 409.) But Collins Denny, Jr., after losing a court battle at the Supreme Court formed the Southern Methodist Church in 1939.

[10]M. W. Clair, Jr., "Methodism and the Negro," in Anderson, ed., *Methodism*, p. 245.

segregation, and segregation is the ugliest way, because it is couched in such pious terms. My friends, what does segregation do for a people? It sets them aside, it labels them, it says that they are not fit to be treated as other people are treated."[11]

The leaders of black Methodists expressed their people's disgust and disappointment and their tenacious opposition. James P. Brawley writes:

> It was the hope of the Negro membership of the Methodist Episcopal Church that his status would be improved in the new United Church and that no structural organization would set him apart and give him less dignity and recognition than he already had . . . He, therefore, rejected the plan of union . . . This was a stigma too humiliating to accept.[12]

There were a few black Methodists who tried to offer what they considered to be moderating or perhaps pragmatic comments suggesting that the Central Jurisdiction would create equal opportunities and powers with the white Jurisdictions. A few others favored it because they saw it as a greater chance in obtaining status in prestigious positions and in exercising leadership for the race under the auspices of The Methodist Church. And a very few favored saving the church embarrassment and withdrawing from the church. Daniel W. Shaw expressed this unpopular view:

> Now, I maintain that we are hindrance to the white people as to organic union with the Church South, and the white people are hindrance to us in the matter of growth and development. I am therefore prepared to ask the next General Conference to appoint a commission to draw up articles of separation and to order a plebiscite on the question of setting the Negroes apart by themselves, with all their church and school property turned over to them in fee simple with an annual stipend of $120,000 reducible at the rate of $10,000 per quadrennium until the sum should be reduced to $50,000, which sum should be permanent or reducible only on the

[11] Culver, *op. cit.*, p. 72.
[12] Brawley, "Methodist Church . . .", p. 4.

motion of the recipient, or on a ratio as suggested above. The terms of the articles of separation shall be so constructed as not to cut us off from either the sympathy or advice of the great Church.

We shall want such a separation as will really make the Negro the initiator and leader in his own Church. We shall want such a separation so as to leave us in good fellowship with our brethren in white, and will make it possible for them to sit in all of our commissions, councils, and conferences and trustee boards, as advisory members. Such a setting apart of our colored people would send a new thrill of life everywhere among us, and we would get a new grip on the colored people of the country and our growth in numbers, and therefore in financial ability would be so marked that we should soon be able to release every dollar of the stipend.[13]

The black leaders rejected the Plan in their vote at General Conference: of the forty-seven delegates, thirty-six voted against the Plan and eleven abstained. But the Plan was overwhelmingly passed by the white delegates. At 8:59 p.m. in Kansas City, Missouri, on May 10 the presiding officer declared that the Declaration of Union had been adopted. It was time for blacks to sit and weep. While others stood up to rejoice, most mourned.

The nineteen Annual Conferences and Black Methodism voted on the Plan later, seven against, two for, and nine abstaining; their fate had already been decided and their future previously charted for them.

The Plan had won, and those blacks who remained were shuttled into the separate corner of the newly "unified" Methodist Church in 1939. Whatever power black Methodists thought they might have gained and were about to share with whites on an equal basis was soon realized as nonexistent. A black bishop was just that—a bishop of blacks and blacks only. It was to be dramatically proven more than twenty years later, when a black bishop of the Methodist

[13]Daniel W. Shaw, "Should the Negroes of the Methodist Episcopal Church Be Set Apart in a Church by Themselves?" Quoted by M. W. Clair, Jr., *op. cit.*, p. 245.

Church tried to enter Garroway Methodist Church, a white church in Jackson, Mississippi, with one of his white fellow-bishops. Even though he was a bishop with Jurisdiction over the same area, he was rudely turned away and reminded that he was a black bishop of black Methodists.

IX

THE DEVELOPMENT OF A CHURCH WITHIN A CHURCH

SANCTIONERS OF THE STATUS QUO

The establishment of the Central Jurisdiction institutionalized a Black Methodist Church. It made visible to the world that Black Methodists were in fact that: *Black* Methodists. It provided the structure for Black Methodists to elect Black bishops to superintend black churches and people and attend to the spiritual affairs of black society. It removed the illusion that The Methodist Church was somehow an inclusive fellowship of Jesus Christ that worshipped a God who is "no respecter of persons." While The Methodist Church continued its traditional and historic pattern of condemning specific social evils and moral wrongs, such as drinking liquor and smoking tobacco, going so far as to force its preachers to vow that they would not partake, segregation and discrimination were beyond the pale. As one of its bishops, the chairman of the Commission from the Southern Church put it: "This philosophy (segregation) of race relations was deep-seated and stronger even than any church affiliations."[1]

The Northern Church provided a well-respected spokesman to deliver the theological basis for the church's position. Albert C. Knudson, then the Dean of Boston University

[1]John W. Morre, *The Long Road to Methodist Union* (Nashville: Abingdon Press, 1943), p. 137.

School of Theology, showed how Christian theology could justify racial segregation:

> *The only basis for denouncing all social separation or segregation as un-Christian is to be found in the theory of racial amalgamation.* (Those who favor amalgamation) think that God made a mistake in creating different races or that he had nothing to do with creation . . .
>
> The theory of racial amalgamation is not a Christian theory.
>
> *The Christian theory is the theory of self-respect, racial self-respect.* It holds that God created the different races, that he had a purpose in so doing, and that each has its contribution to make toward the total life of mankind, not through racial elimination, but through racial education and self-development in the divine purpose to be realized . . .
>
> The Christian view of God as Creator leads us to look with reverence and respect upon every race, and *especially upon the race in whose bosom God has given us life . . .*[2]

The Dean of Boston University obviously had not learned that race in itself has no intrinsic value. "When race is used to classify people *socially*, when race is used as a *symbol to set people apart for differential treatment*, the term, with all its inaccuracies, becomes a weapon."[3] This appears to be a clear case of race being used as weapon. What is more intriguing about his statement is that standing alone and apart from his intention, little fault can be found in the affirmation he makes. God did, indeed, make every being to be proud of the blessings of his or her features, but not to place a value on them above the features of others. Knudson, however, by supporting such a stance is saying that God supports oppression of races, not through racial elimination, which Knudson incorrectly sees as the opposite of racial separation, but by racial segregation and thus superiority of one group over another. God as Creator, he asserts, may look upon every race but he does so *especially* upon the one "in whose bosom"

---

[2] Quoted in Culver, *op. cit.*, p. 73. Italics added.

[3] William B. McClain, Travelling Light: *Christian Perspectives on Pilgrimage and Pluralism* (New York: Friendship Press, 1981), p. 34. See pp. 31–34 for a discussion on "The Mis-Use of 'Race' and 'Ethnicity.' "

they themselves feel he resides only.[4] Obviously, it did not occur to Dean Knudson that the *racial self-respect* which he commends had been destroyed for Black Methodists by setting them apart with less dignity than they already had through the implicit suggestion that they were not "fit to be treated as other people are treated."

In setting up the Central Jurisdiction The Methodist Church capitulated to the countercurrents of American racist proclivities, and yielded to the prevailing morality of the society. Its ethics became those temporal pragmatic considerations of the world rather than the eternal claims of justice which its prophetic Lord had declared. No longer was the church willing to challenge the culture to see itself as a *reformer* of culture on racial matters; rather, it became *one* with the prevailing culture. It became the American Church reflecting the attitudes and practices of the larger society. Its faith was co-opted. It became a group under the regulations, manipulations, and maneuvers of economic, cultural, political, and social forces. The sectarian heritage of Methodism was lost to an engulfing institutionalism. It became imbued with the desire to be accepted and to find a ready companionship with those in power. Rather than subverting evils in society or in the church, Methodists became sanctioners of the status quo with all its inequities; rather than promoting wholeness or holiness and sanctification for others, The Methodist Church became bent on pious and sanctimonious utterances which covered up the real issues which beckoned its public witness. It succumbed to the principalities and powers.

THE INVISIBLE CHURCH:
ITS MEANING AND AMBIVALENCE

The "invisible church" had always been there—dating back to the separate prayer meetings, the brush arbor experiences, the preaching of Black Harry and Henry Evans and

[4]See *Ibid.*, pp. 71–75 for a summary theological discussion of racial separation as sin.

other sons of thunder, the creation of the Negro spiritual, and a religion the slaves had transformed and made their own. Its worship style had combined secular relevance with deep spirituality in a context of simplicity and informality— taking only from the white church what was necessary to contribute to survival with dignity.

Its worship had never been a retreat from the agonies and ecstacies of life. Rather, it had been the experience of a people who lived on the existential edge where the creative and the destructive, the wise and the foolish, the sacred and the secular, the agony and the ecstacy, *the up and the down* were the contrarieties of human existence witnessed in the presence of the divine. The essence of its tradition was the extraordinary tension between the poles of pain and joy, Saturday night and Sunday morning. It was the worship of the disinherited and dispossessed.

Even in those places where there was the emulation of the white churches and their worship style, "Amazing Grace" never quite sounded the same, and there was a bit of a "bounce" in the choir's procession. The black religious experience had meticulously placed some chords in the soul that were responsive to its familiar beat. No yearning thought of assimilation could totally drown out the sound of the pulsing jungle: faint, perhaps, but still there. And as the preacher recalled the experience of "coming over a way that with tears has been watered," even in affected accent, a terrible paroxysm of pain was felt in the heart. For even then the stentorian words of a prophet could be heard over the hills of history by a sensitive and suffering people: "Take away from me the noise of your songs; to the melody of your harp I will not listen. But let justice roll down like water, and righeousness like a mighty stream."

No, the establishment of the Central Jurisdiction did not create the Black Methodist "invisible church," it merely made it an *organizational reality*. It made structurally manifest what was a latent reality. It gave sanction without autonomy. It reinforced the two-mindedness[5] of Black Methodists in particular who were often forced to hang their heads in shame as they tried to defend the existence of the Central Jurisdiction as an institution of Black Americans. That is, in part, why all sat and some wept when they were told their fate. The problem of ambivalence which nagged most of the institutions of Black Americans could not be escaped by being black in The Methodist Church. This double-consciousness was made more painfully apparent with the existence of the Central Jurisdiction.

Be it ever so true that blacks in other black churches were also separated from their white Christian brothers and sisters who claimed allegiance to the same Lord, and were victims of racial segregation and discrimination in the society in general, there were also taunts from other black churches that the blacks in The Methodist Church were members of a "Jim Crow" church which would not allow them to fully participate in the life and work of the church. Some had predicted that their minority status was ever to be "a mere cipher."[6] Their continued presence in The Methodist Church was seen as a lack of independence and an inability to be self-supporting.

THE GOALS OF THE CENTRAL JURISDICTION

As the Black Methodists began their work as the Central Jurisdiction, a church within a church—the invisible made visible—there were at least two prevailing attitudes that influenced its work and its perception of itself. One was to

---

[5]This refers to W. E. B. DuBois' classic statement. "One ever feels his twoness—as American, a Negro; two souls, two thoughts, two unreconciled strivings; two warring ideals in one dark body, who dogged strength alone keeps it from being torn asunder." *Souls of Black Folk in Three Negro Classics* (New York: Avon Books, 1965), p. 215.

[6]Bishop Daniel A. Payne of the African Methodist Church is quoted in W. J. Walls, *The African Methodist Episcopal Zion Church* (Charlotte, North Carolina: A.M.E. Zion Publishing House, 1974), pp. 242f.

accept the reality of the Central Jurisdiction and use it as a vehicle of advantage for the whole of black society. The second was to work within its limits, but always toward the hope that it would be an interim step toward a more inclusive church; where Methodism would realize its potential as the multi-racial fellowship in which all barriers based exclusively on racial and color distributions, at every level of the church, would be eliminated and Methodism would become a truly inclusive company of the people of God.

When the Central Jurisdiction gathered for its first meeting in St. Louis, Missouri, in 1940, Bishop Robert E. Jones in his episcopal address tried to assess the total situation. In pointing out the actual advantages Black Methodists had in the Central Jurisdiction, he said in part:

> . . . We gain the privilege of electing our own bishops who at once become full members of the Council of Bishops with the same status of bishops similarly elected . . .
>
> We of the Central Jurisdiction of The Methodist Church have an advantage for the promotion of interracial Christian brotherhood which is not held by any other religious group of people . . . It therefore behooves us at the very beginning of our career as a separate jurisdiction to recognize the gravity of our responsibility as well as the favorableness of our opportunity. It is a responsibility we should by no means shirk; and *it is an opportunity of which we should hasten to take every advantage.*[7]

Indeed, black bishops were elected to superintend the work of the five areas and Liberia, West Africa, as well as the Black Methodist Churches throughout the Central Jurisdiction—an immense geographical area which included the boundaries of the nineteen Annual Conferences discussed earlier, plus the work of the Conference already established in Liberia, West Africa. The fourteen men elected to serve as episcopal leaders of the Central Jurisdiction during its existence performed their duties with varying degrees of distinction. While the Black Methodist local churches did not keep

[7]See J. B. F. Shaw, *The Negro in the History of Methodism* (Nashville: Parthenon Press, 1954), pp. 189ff. for the entire episcopal address. Italics added.

pace in membership growth with the white jurisdictions, nevertheless they showed growth each quadrennium. Growth was affected by the migration pattern from the South (where the great majority of Black Methodist Churches were located) into other sections of the country; either where some Black Methodist Churches were beginning to transfer to the jurisdiction where they were located, under changed legislation of 1956 which allowed local churches of the Central Jurisdiction to effect such transfers, or Black Methodists were moving to areas where there were no Black Methodist Churches.

Black institutions of higher learning were supported by the black annual conferences and made stronger, receiving accreditation from their regional accrediting agencies. The schools continued to provide trained leadership, both lay and clergy, for the Black Methodist Church and the black community. Gammon Theological Seminary year after year produced theologically-trained clergymen to serve the local black churches and institutions of the black community. It boasted in 1960 of having graduated twelve hundred persons. Among its alumni were twenty college presidents, thirty college professors, fifteen bishops (nine in The Methodist Church and six in other denominations), fifty-four military chaplains, ten editors of church periodicals, and numerous local pastors trained to serve the church as professional clergypersons. In addition, Gammon became the nucleus for a merger of several black theological seminaries to form the Interdenominational Theological Center in Atlanta with aid from the two Rockefeller Foundations.

The Central Jurisdiction "hastened to take every advantage" of its separate existence and serve Black Methodists. Efforts were made to enrich worship experiences, upgrade church parsonages and church facilities, recruit and train more lay and clergy leaders, increase and enliven the work of women's groups. And there was help from the national church to support the efforts of the Black Methodists of the Central Jurisdiction.

The second attitude prevailing in the Central Jurisdiction was committed to agitate and keep the pressure on the general church to *eliminate* the Central Jurisdiction and make The Methodist Church an inclusive fellowship. Bishop Alexander P. Shaw expressed this concern in 1944:

> We are not in harmony with any Methodists or others who think such a plan necessary in a truly Christian brotherhood. We consider it expedient only on account of the Christian childhood of some American Methodists who need a little cuddling until they can grow into full grown manhood and womanhood in Christ Jesus. We are hopeful that in the very near future our Methodism may become sufficiently Christian in character and maturity to find a more excellent way.[8]

Ralph A. Felton expressed sharply the disappointment of those who continued to believe that Methodism had in its heart, somewhere in its power, the ability to wean men and women of their racist attitudes and rid The Methodist Church of its segregated structure. In a study of the Central Jurisdiction from 1941 to 1951 he wrote:

> Each four years since 1940 as General Conference approaches, the debate is renewed about doing away with this segregated Jurisdiction . . . After General Conference adjourns, courteous silence reigns again.[9]

A STEP TOWARD INCLUSIVENESS

Events outside of the Church intensified the racial issue: World War II focusing on Nazism, the founding of the United Nations as an international human rights organization, the establishing of the World Council of Churches and its concern for world ecumenism and world problems, the 1954 Supreme Court decision outlawing segregation, and the civil rights movement removing barriers in the larger society.

---

[8]*Journal of the Jurisdictional Conference of The Methodist* Church, 1944, pp. 52–67. Cited in Graham, *op. cit.,* pp. 91–92.

[9]Ralph A. Felton, *The Ministry of the Central Jurisdiction of The Methodist Church* (Madison, New Jersey: Drew University Theological Seminary, 1965), p. 26.

These events and others on the outside combined with pressure on the inside from Black Methodists *and a few others* at each quadrennial Conference made it difficult for the Church to fail to act. Commissions and committees were appointed to study the situation of minorities in the church and the jurisdictional system, especially the Central Jurisdiction. In 1956, the General Conference approved an instrument to facilitate the abolition of the Central Jurisdiction. Amendment IX was added to the Constitution of The Methodist Church permitting transfer of churches to other annual conferences, provided it had prior approval by the quarterly conference (local church) and the two annual conferences involved.

The Central Jurisdiction expressed itself through the Committee of Five and a study conference convened March 26–28, 1961, in Cincinnati, Ohio. Its report, *Central Jurisdiction Speaks*, developed the following principles:

1. The fundamental objective in the dissolution of the Central Jurisdiction must be *de facto* inclusiveness in the Methodist Church.
2. The minimum requirement of *de facto* inclusiveness is the absence on all levels of church life of patterns and policies based on race or color.
3. Each step taken to dissolve the Central Jurisdiction must be an integral part of an overall plan to abolish all forms of racial segregation and discrimination from the Methodist Church.[10]

In 1966, The Methodist Church, after much agony, pressure and a combination of many events and factors (including merger with the Evangelical United Brethren Church) set a date for the termination of the Central Jurisdiction. The Plan for Union with the Evangelical United Brethren Church, unlike the earlier Plan of Union of 1939, did not

[10]*Central Jurisdiction Speaks*, 1961, pp. 8–9. Cited in Graham, *op. cit.*, pp. 98–99. John H. Graham served on the Committee of Five along with James S. Thomas, Chairman; Richard Erwin, W. Astor Kirk and John J. Hicks.

provide for the Central Jurisdiction to continue. It died a slow death.

A few Black Methodists made some futile efforts to prolong its life, but the decision of the body that created it prevailed in its demise.

X

BLACK METHODISTS:
A Remnant or a Residue

ASSIMILATION: A DREAM DEFERRED

The death of the Central Jurisdiction did not achieve what its "killers" expected—or at least what the Black Methodists who participated were seeking. As is true in the larger society, and has been proven over and over again, ending *de jure* segregation does not necessarily produce *de facto* integration. Many Black Methodists had not learned what Malcolm X understood: "It appears that many people who seem to be asking 'What can I do?' actually are asking 'What can I do without changing anything?' " Malcolm appropriately and correctly answered, "Nothing!" The racism, which had so pervaded this society and to which The Methodist Church succumbed in establishing The Black Methodist Church in the first place, merely reappeared in other areas of process and structures and took on other forms.

Black Methodists of the Central Jurisdiction had as their fundamental objective and intention in dissolving the Central Jurisdiction *de facto* inclusiveness. They defined "*de facto* inclusiveness" as "the absence on all levels of church life of patterns and policies based on color."[1] No such inclusiveness yet has occurred in any significant way. With the elimination of the Central Jurisdiction in 1968, the struggle for Black Methodists simply shifted. Technically, they were included

[1] *Ibid.*

in the whole structure of the denomination, and not isolated by law into separate Annual Conferences. They were able to secure all the rights, benefits, and privileges afforded to all Methodists who follow its creed and vows of membership. A number of blacks received appointments to executive jobs that blacks had never occupied before; a few cross-race appointments were made for a few "over-qualified" black pastors to less-than-prestigious white churches; black bishops were elected by majority—white jurisdictional bodies—in some cases blacks whom blacks would never have elected in the Central Jurisdiction where they chose their leadership; and a number of blacks were elected to offices and appointed as district superintendents; but *de facto* inclusiveness has not yet occurred.

Ten years after the decision to dissolve the Central Jurisdiction, Grant S. Shockley and others did a wide-ranging and revealing study of the state of the church in 1976. Under the able research leadership of Shockley, the former President of Interdenominational Theological Center, the project secured from district superintendents some information about the ethnic and racial characteristics of the church members and pastors. A survey instrument was developed and mailed out directly to all known black clergy in the United Methodist Church—including pastors, district superintendents, ministers in special appointments, beyond the local church and a sample of white pastors. The report concludes:

> United Methodism has accepted the notion of "inclusive fellowship" but seems unclear about the radicality of the ethics it invokes and unwilling to actualize the behavior it demands. Guided by such a partial ethic, United Methodism over the past ten years had *identified structural desegregation with "inclusiveness" and redistributed rather than dissolved the former Central Jurisdiction.*[2]

What was made visible in the Central Jurisdiction and predecessant organizational arrangements was made invis-

[2] Grant Shockley *et al.*, *Black Pastors and Churches in United Methodism* (Atlanta: Center for Research in Social Change, Emory University, 1976), p. 2. Italics added.

ible again—a church within a church, distributed in different places. The report goes on to suggest the root of the problem: "the inability (on the part of white Methodism) to practice genuine Christian fellowship with black people."[3]

What is clear is that Black Methodists, the largest color minority in any Protestant denomination in America, found themselves in an ambiguous position in 1976; unassimilated into the larger body and without independence as a Black Church. "A decade of so-called interracial mergers" had not significantly altered the "inclusive" profile of the church beyond tokenism.[4] Methodism was not prepared to accept the cultural diversity which Black Methodists represented, and it was unwilling to seriously confront the question of interdependence with its largest minority. The inclusiveness which was sought was not forthcoming. Obviously, genuine inclusion which involves both equal opportunity and equal advantage was not the intent of those who voted with the Black Methodists to abolish the Central Jurisdiction. The controlling structure of the church—even though it required no new legislation—was unwilling to practice an open pastoral itinerancy beyond the tokenism referred to earlier.

At a more fundamental level, the church really lives out its life of faith, witness, and service at the local level, in the community, where relations are more personal, communal, and voluntary. Methodists are not a structure, they are the people who join local churches, gather for worship, live in communities and act out their faith in the society. Some would even go so far as to say that "the local church is where the action is." In any case, the Shockley study points out the real situation at the local church level, "In spite of more than a decade of efforts toward merger and integration, *most black members are in black churches and most white members are in all-white churches.*"[5]

---

[3] *Ibid.*
[4] *Ibid.*
[5] *Ibid.*, p. 3. The study provides illuminating tables to document this conclusion. See pp. 14–15 for Tables 3 and 4.

It is quite clear that at the voluntary level there is no trend toward inclusive fellowship. United Methodist Churches are, by and large, homogenous. As yet, there is no significant indication that there is any movement to change this pattern.

THE DILEMMA FACING BLACK METHODISM TODAY

It was perhaps in part the realization of these realities and the absence of an organized structure for Black Methodists that led to the formation of Black Methodists for Church Renewal in 1968. In their *Black Paper,* after making confession about the failure to be "reconciled with ourselves as black men" and "honest with ourselves and with our white brothers," Black Methodists stated their intent about their mission as Black Methodists and added a statement about their relationship and commitment to the United Methodist Church: "We hope this can be done within the new framework of the United Methodist Church. As for Black Methodists, we are determined to serve God by redeeming our brothers, which in turn redeems us."[6]

The position Black Methodists could not agree among themselves to say was, "within or outside The United Methodist Church." The debate was long and heated. The overriding sentiment was that their continued presence in the organization could force, pressure, shame, or prod the Church to change; to rediscover its historic *raison d'être* and to stand against racism and the powerlessness of black people in America as it had done against slavery at the Baltimore Conference of 1780 and its founding Christmas Conference at Lovely Lane in 1784. The realization of this view remains yet to be seen.

In 1969, Gilbert Caldwell's article in *The Christian Century,* aptly entitled "Black Folk in White Churches", expressed the hopes and frustrated dreams of Black Methodists, Black Christians in white denominations, and, perhaps, Black peo-

---

[6] "The Black Paper" in *Findings of Black Methodists for Church Renewal,* 1968.

ple in general who harbor some hope in the Christian Church: "Thank God for my own Black Methodists for Church Renewal. I have the feeling that if these structures [Black caucuses in white denominations] had not emerged a lot of us would have received 'calls' to preach in places other than the church."[7] He goes further to state the double-consciousness which is specifically present in Black Methodists, and in Black people in general in whatever other structures.

> There is a ray of hope—not that we see our white brothers getting ready for us, but rather that through such structures as black caucuses we are beginning to see in clear terms that ours is a dual responsibility: to minister not only to the people in our communities but also to our white brothers and sisters.[8]

Whether Black Methodists for Church Renewal has accomplished the latter task is not clear. It may have become so institutionalized and co-opted by the agenda of those who seek movement into the coveted positions beyond the local church that it has lost its initial thrust to be the "gadfly" of the white church. Its prophetic vision has been dimmed by the near-sightedness of those who see only the small achievements which require no radical change in the United Methodist Church. The organization's agenda appears to bring together only black lay people and clergy who see themselves as people who ought to be a part of the process of decision making and view its meetings as a way to express their alienation—a catharsis and a way to re-live the old, and perhaps relieve the continuing pain of what is and the resignation to what is not.

But the former task is accomplished by Black Methodists for Church Renewal and other gatherings where Black Methodists come together: the ambiguous becomes clear,

---

[7]Gilbert H. Caldwell, "Black Folk in White Churches," reprinted in *The Black Experience in Religion*, ed. by C. Eric Lincoln (Garden City, New York: Anchor Books, 1974), p. 29.

[8]*Ibid.*, pp. 29–30.

the invisible becomes visible, the unstated becomes stated. Black Methodists let down the guards and black people become black people again—not just Black Methodists—but the people they hoped Methodism could embrace and discover: A people with a rich tradition and an ability to make sense of the true spirit of Methodism, as its roots knew, a God who sides with the poor and the oppressed, and whose requirements of justice threaten those who choose temporal ethics over the eternal absolutes.

The Black Methodist Church as a church within United Methodism becomes visible at these gatherings and takes on the characteristics of every other Black Church. The theology reflected in the speeches, sermons, resolutions, and discussions is not merely the rarefied abstractions of the academy, nor the Gnosticism of learned European scholars; but talk about a God who hears the cries of the oppressed and the dispossessed and whose nostrils are sickened by the stench and filth of racism and bigotry. They talk of a God whose Calvary hill is higher than Capitol Hill and whose love reaches into the ghettoes of the cities and the sharecropper's farms of the Mississippi Delta. The worship services at these gatherings become the familiar sound of a people caught in captivity singing the Songs of Zion in a strange land. The overt emotionalism, often frowned upon in other places, is expressed without apology or shame. The preaching takes on a familiar cadence, the rhetoric and speech of those whose errand is urgent and whose sound is certain and untentative. Class loses distinction. Those who are caught in bourgeois captivity and a spectrum of values which sets them apart from the masses, mingle in spirit and body with their lesser educated and economically fixed brothers and sisters as they join together as the Black Methodist Church.

At these periodically planned gatherings—becoming more frequent the farther behind in history the Central Jurisdiction is—the invisible church becomes visible and intentionally so. Frequent trips are made to Gammon Theological Seminary, the Mecca of Black Methodism. Consultations are planned to remind the Black Methodists of their distinct and different history, and spiritual revitalization takes place to keep members functioning in a Church controlled by the majority population.

The question Black Methodists may have to answer for themselves is whether those who remained in the United Methodist Church are a faithful remnant upon whom the future existence of the United Methodist Church in becoming a truly inclusive fellowship depends—the bearers of promise and the hope for reformation, or whether they are simply a sedimental residue—merely what is left over at the end of a painful process with sentimental memories of the past and how it could have been and should have been different.

APPENDIX I

This Address was given May 17, 1980 at the Harry Hoosier Annual Banquet, Philadelphia, Pennsylvania. This is a yearly observance sponsored by the Black United Methodist Preachers of Philadelphia in honor of the illustrious Black Harry Hoosier, one among them in the founding of the church.

A Theologial Dilemma:
Racism As Sin

It is altogether fitting and proper that Black Methodists gather at a banquet in the City of Philadelphia under the name Harry Hoosier. For it was he who first introduced Methodism to the eloquence, passion, and fire of black preaching. It is even more marvelous that this unlettered son of thunder who traveled with the learned Dr. Thomas Coke and the pioneering Bishop Francis Asbury and others was more popular than they. It is reported that when someone inquired about his illiteracy he said: "I sing by faith, pray by faith and do everything by faith; without faith in Jesus Christ I can do nothing." That is truly a testimony of faith and the words of one who took seriously the words of Paul: "I can do all things through him who strengthens me."

"Black Harry," as he was often called, has never received from the historians of Methodism the place he deserves in the annals of the history of Methodism. Even as we approach the bicentennial of the Christmas Conference at Lovely Lane Chapel the legend of this unlettered genius of the pioneer church and the mystery of this charismatic character continues to haunt historians.

And so it is altogether fitting and proper that we gather together tonight to celebrate his work and ministry and extol the virtues and contributions of a dynamic black servant of God who used his tongue to preach redemption to the captors and the captives.

The very church that Hoosier helped to establish and to expand is yet today, almost 200 years after its apprenticeship in the Christian religion still plagued by the insidious disease that prevented him from being credited for his accomplishments and received fully as a being of inestimable worth. That disease is racism.

For too long in the Christian Church racism has not been perceived for what it is—a basic theological problem. The problem of race is at its deepest level not a factual problem, nor a moral problem, but a theological problem.

Let me try to suggest some reasons why racism is a theological problem, comment upon those and suggest some Christian responses.

Racism is a theological problem because it is sin. It is not merely a moral error, an error in judgment, or a social aberration. It is sin because it divides the human family and blurs the image of God in persons.

We are created in the image of God. We possess what the theologians call *the imago dei*—the image of God. This means that God has bestowed upon each person his mark, made them in his image and called all persons to the same destiny. It cannot be decided by looking at people; we must look at God. God alone is the source of human dignity. God has created all in the image of himself and herein lies their dignity. It is not an achievement or a merit or even an intrinsic quality. It is a gift, a bestowal.

The Christian faith affirms that there is an essential unity of humankind. It is therein we find contained our essential likeness to God and our likeness to each other. To divide what God has made as a unity and to blur that image by judging persons by the color of their skin is to commit sin against God. Racism does that. It calls into question God's creative action. For what it implies is that God has made a creative error in bringing into being the races other than white.

It is in the act of creation itself that equality is achieved. This does not suggest that all persons are equal in intelligence, capacity, skill, knowledge, or talent. Few of us can preach with the eloquence of Hoosier—even with years of seminary training in speech, elocution and homiletics. It means that persons can claim rights to be equal as persons, as creatures of God. These are rights that belong to every person by merely being persons created in the image of God. This right exists prior to any achievement, merit or performance of any function. It is a basic and primary right—an inalienable right as recognized by the framers of the Declaration of Independence. But it existed even before they recognized it. It is part of the order of creation. It is an imperative of love from the Creator.

The Declaration of Independence, in stating "All men are created equal" was simply a statement of a truth in a democratic political document that the biblical faith had discovered and dogmatized long before it: "He hath created of one blood all men to dwell on the face of the earth." To deny that in acts of racism and oppression is to be in conflict with God—the very essence of sin.

Racism is sin because the racists rely on race as a source of their personal value. Their lives have meaning and worth because they are part of the racial context. To quote the old Prophet Habakkuk: "Dread and terrible are they; their justice and dignity proceed from themselves." (Habakkuk 1:7). When a person relies on himself for his ultimate worth he "thinks of himself more highly than he ought to think." This leads to a worship of self rather than God. The Creator is replaced by the creature. That is the original sin of pride. This is self-love as opposed to mutual love.

I am speaking of racism and not racial consciousness, racial prejudice or class oppression. Let me draw the difference.

Prejudice means an unfavorable opinion, feeling or attitude formed beforehand without knowledge, thought or reason. Prejudice involves prejudgment and misjudgment of a human group. Presumably this could be corrected by learning and experience. But racism involves having the *power* to carry out the prejudices, whether personally or institutionally. Racism means subordinating persons or groups because of their color. It is not simply a matter of attitude. It is a matter of enacting one's will over another. And power makes the difference. The process of control of whites over non-whites is built into the major social institutions of our society.

There is a difference between racial consciousness and racism. Race consciousness emerges out of the need to classify and the search for group identity. It contains the potential for racism because like all knowledge it portends alienation. But it only becomes racism when it is perverted. That is, when one views others and oneself in terms of color in a closed, rigid view of the relation between race and behavior, race and character, race and virtue, race and intelligence—then race consciousness becomes racism. Race consciousness becomes racism when it becomes associated with relations between and among persons based on the oppression of one group by another.

It is neither racial consciousness or racial prejudice that I am talking about. It is racism and its insidious tentacles that reach into every area of human life that I am suggesting is still the major problem in American society and is a serious theological problem for the Christian Church.

Our recent General Conference of the United Methodist Church [1980] grappled with this problem somewhat in a lesser degree than necessary to eradicate it and to extirpate it from the Church. But at least we adopted a Charter at the insistence of the Women's Division. But in order to rid ourselves of this heinous evil and colossal sin a total commitment must be made. Certainly the priority of the Ethnic

Minority Local Church is a step in the right direction. But it will require the involvement and commitment of all.

Many prefer to see the problem of racism and its accompanying evils of poverty, ethnic oppression and cultural imperialism as matters outside of the purview of their personal concern. While they may accept equality as generally a good thing, what is lacking is a sense of the monstrosity of inequality. They fail to see the widening gap between the income of whites and blacks, the great discrepancy between unemployment of the black and hispanic community and that of the white community, the steady and constant erosion of quality education in urban schools, and the growing rate of crime in the black community fed and fostered by deteriorating social conditions. That failure to see leads to an indifference to evil and injustice. Perhaps seeing the solutions to these problems as platitudes, they prefer to remain neutral, impartial and unmoved by the extremity of these evils. Such indifference to evil is even more insidious than evil itself; it is more widespread, more contagious and highly more dangerous. To be silent and unconcerned gives a tacit justification for these evils. It makes possible these evils erupting as exceptions becoming the rule and thereby being accepted. Such a case allows for persons to be decent but sinister, pious but sinful. Instead of these problems being a scandal to the heart they are seen as social conditions resulting from the way things are.

Part of the problem is that justice and equality are perceived by most of the majority population as an idea, or a norm, a good social goal. It would be good if it obtained, but it is seen as a goal, a utopian idea. But in the eyes of the prophets and in the eyes of Jesus justice was not seen as an idea or a norm. This is not what the prophet Amos had in mind when he thundered: "Let justice roll down like waters and righteousness like a mightly stream." (Amos 5:24). Justice is charged with the omnipotence of God. It is a mighty stream, expressive of the vehemence of a never-ending, surging, fighting movement—washing away obstacles as its mighty waters roll down. "The mountain falls, and crumbles away, the rock is removed from its place—the waters wear away the stone." (Job 14:18ff) It is not merely a utopian idea nor even a desirable norm, but a restless drive empowered by an omnipotent God. What ought to be, must be!

We are the black church, born out of the wound of struggle. We are charged with continuing the fight for justice and freedom and liberation which our Master began. We must sound the message of liberation which gives rise to hope. To those who are caught in the webs of poverty, whose lives are threatened daily by the insidious tentacles of white power and oppression and whose existence is marked by the struggle against the sin and the consequences of the sin of racism, there is hope. That hope arises out of accepting the liberating promises of God. God is present in Jesus enabling the poor and the oppressed to live in the present in freedom from fear of death while he joins them in establishing a future that is different from the present.

There is present in black history and religion as Harry Hoosier must have known, an indomitable faith in the future.

In our forebears' encounter with Jesus Christ they received a new vision in which a new knowledge of their own personhood enabled them to fight for the creation of a new world. It enabled them to sing, "There is a bright side, somewhere; don't you rest until you find it." This faith in the future, growing out of their liberating encounter with Jesus Christ, energized their hope and prevented that hope from being simply an idle waiting. It enabled an oppressed people to live as if that vision of the future is already realized in the present. This vision of the future held a people together mentally as they struggled physically to make real the future in their present. Our message must recapture that vision. For people cannot live without hope. Without hope the people perish.

Our message must be, as Harry's was, that "without faith in Jesus Christ I can do nothing." That is the same Jesus who

identifies with rat-bitten children in roach-infested tene-
ments and dope addict fathers whose arms are scarred from
the use of dull needles in nasty stinking alleys in Philadelphia. He identifies with struggling sharecroppers in the hot
dusty fields of Mississippi. That same Jesus identifies with
youths whose dreams have been murdered by inadequate
school systems and racist and bigoted teachers. He identifies
with the unemployed whose lives are spent in hopelessness
and despair. He identifies with the frolicking and delusioned
young adults who experience joy with contradiction. To the
confused he gives his peace; to the hate-filled he gives his
love; to those with torn lives he gives his purpose; to the
sorrowful he gives his joy; to the despairing he gives his
hope. He is the One crucified on Calvary and yet the Living
Christ available to the world as the Savior. It is he we offer as
Harry Hoosier did.

> *I sing by faith, pray by faith,*
> *and do everything by faith;*
> *without faith in Jesus Christ*
> *I can do nothing.*

APPENDIX II

Author's Personal Note: This report was prepared for the Board of Global Ministries in 1975 by a Task Force consisting of Ignacio Castuera, Claremont School of Theology; William B. McClain, Pastor of Union United Methodist Church, Boston; and Roy I. Sano, Associate Professor of Theology and Pacific and Asian-American Ministries, Pacific School of Religion. All three members of the Task Force are now in new ministries in The United Methodist Church.

It is reprinted here because of its unique relevance to the questions before the Bicentennial General Conference of the Church and its peculiar appropriateness to this book. It represents the thinking of three ethnic minority ministers of United Methodism (Hispanic, Black and Asian) in 1975 and their own efforts to deal with being "a church within a church"; but more than that, this author found a new health in the fellowship with people who were different who have enriched his life and continue to offer that same kind of enrichment to the Church. We met as virtual strangers; we departed from the task as faithful friends. We continue to be so; no, more so. We discovered that Charles Wesley's prayer can be a good intercession for the whole church:

> Help us to help each other, Lord,
> Each other's cross to bear;
> Let each his friendly aid afford,
> And feel his brother's care.

We approached our task, united by his grace, and found that that was enough. Some others have found it. It is available to the whole church and the whole world.

BIBLICAL AND THEOLOGICAL FOUNDATIONS

for

RACIAL AND ETHNIC MINORITY PERSONS IN MISSION

by

WILLIAM B. MCCLAIN
ROY I. SANO
IGNACIO CASTUERA

1975

(Revised, 1979)

INTRODUCTION

As we undertook the assignment given to us, the Task Force found itself practicing a style of Christian living which combines action and reflection. At the same time we were building a community, conducting investigations, and exploring new options, we found ourselves reflecting on several questions.

1. By what authority do we speak?
2. On what grounds do we focus on the problems of racism in the church, and how do we interpret it?
3. Is there something that can be done, and if so, how do we do it?

Answers to these questions enabled us to do our own work. They also surfaced the faith which sustains and guides. Although this faith which we share with all Christians should express itself in symbols and categories from other cultures as well, we found the familiar and traditional resources could serve us well for the present task.

AUTHORITY: THE RIGHT TO PROCEED, RESOURCES, AND METHODS

First, concerning the authority by which this Task Force can speak on problems within the church. Besides the more immediate mandate which the Board of Global Ministries granted the Inter-Ethnic Task Force, we see ourselves fulfilling the priority set by Jesus himself when he challenged his disciples to learn how to "interpret the signs of the times" rather than reading the "appearances of earth and sky." (Matthew 16:3 and Luke 12:56) The resources (authority and perspective) for our interpretations have been found in what John Wesley called the "four corners," namely, the Bible, tradition, experience and reason. When we reflect upon our experiences as ethnic minorities in the programs of Persons in Mission we are led by the Bible and tradition to begin with the theme of judgment. As the writer of the Petrine letters states, "The time has come for judgment to begin in the household of God." (1Peter 4:17)

CREATION, THE FALL AND RACISM

The second question asks for the reason behind this focus on racism and whether it is a problem which should concern Christians? For answers to these questions we call attention to the resources of the Christian understanding of Creation and the Fall. They translate what is happening into issues which Christians are obligated to address. Stated briefly, our common understanding of Creation validates the Pronouncements the church has made; our shared experiences of the Fall explain the Performances. We conclude that we have violated the goodness of God's creation.

The Pronouncements follow the pattern of God's deeds and words recalled in the creation stories. (Genesis 1) Everything created by God is called "good." Even more, when the creation of humankind is assessed, the Creator says it is "very good."

Eco-Justice can be interpreted to mean justice to the whole ecology, both human as well as natural. All creatures, great and small, have the right to fulfillment of their potentials, a right to make their distinctive contributions. This Report highlights the right of ethnic minorities within the Body of Christ. They are the descendants of the Third World peoples who presently constitute two-thirds of the world.

If the Church had not spoken explicitly an affirmative word concerning ethnic minorities in the family of God, and a positive word concerning their contributions to the Household of Faith, we would have committed the sin of omission. When Christians are silent on these points they have spoken the Word of God less fully than they would like to think no matter how biblical they claim to be. Fortunately, the United Methodist Church has had faithful witnesses to the Word of God. They have helped us say with the Psalmist, "The earth is the Lord's and the fullness thereof, the world, and those who dwell therein." (Psalms 24:1)

If the doctrine of Creation validates the Pronouncements, the insights of our tradition embodied in the doctrine of the Fall explain the disparity between Pronouncements and Performances. The goodness of creation has gone awry and humankind has played a critical role in the death which ensues. (Romans 5) The irony is that the very attempt to avert death seals its certainty in human experience. (Genesis 3)

We see "original (or, fundamental) sin" as a preoccupation with the self induced by the fear of death. In classical terms, sin is an involvement of a person with self or a preoccupation of people with themselves. When we recognize the boundaries of our finitude and creatureliness, we are tempted to extend our selfhood beyond their God-given limits in space and time. (Genesis 3:3–4) We resort to various avenues, including efforts to reproduce copies of ourselves in other people so that we can go on living through them. We define for them what we have discovered for ourselves is true, good and beautiful. We give an aura of divine sanction to our values and views, dressing them in religious vestments. If we go unchallenged, we will announce that our values are God's Law and our views are God's Word, for all people. By doing so, we prevent other people from making their unique contributions to the full tapestry of God's creation. We thwart their development. We promote death, and not the flowering and fruitation of other forms of life and styles of living. One denomination can do this to other views of faith, whites can do this to people of color, and males can do this to women.

If we claim we live above this propensity, we fulfill the prophecy of Pascal. "Humankind is neither angel nor brute, and when they try to be angels they become brutes." *(Or see 1 John 1:10)* The claims of religious people that they do not succumb to this temptation to be gods creating others in their image makes their practices of it all the more insidious. No wonder Jesus levelled his severest attacks against the Pharisees and called them "whited sepulchers." (Matthew 23–27) Their customs and laws produced oppressive tombs, prompting death not life. No wonder the greater bulk of the Pauline letters in the New Testament directs an attack upon the Judaisers, the early representatives of a (culture-bound) Christianity which attempted to impose their laws on others. From this perspective the high points in our Christian heritage occur in Augustine, Luther and John Wesley when they challenged the bondage of legally defined conditions for God's acceptance.

BIFURCATIONS AND BOXES

As ethnic minorities in the United Methodist Church we have seen contemporary versions of the Pharisees and Judaisers. We have not heard the Good News of God's acceptance and liberation from "whited sepulchers," despite the claims to the contrary. Guidelines and Laws have been laid in our pathway before we enter the inner sanctuaries.

They appear in what we are calling in this Report the bifurcations and the boxes. The bifurcations appear in the "either/
or" options which have dominated the appeals of conten-
tious parties within the church which have recruited us. We
were told by some that salvation is personal and inward,
while others told us it was social and outward. Some said the
ultimate value was spiritual, while others said the term
"spiritual" was a "dirty word" [Sir George McCleod] and
that Christianity was "the most materialistic religion the
world has ever known" [Archbishop William Temple]. Some
claim genuine Christian outreach is evangelistic, while
others claim it involves social action. Some predicted we
would find God in the movements of the world (immanence
of God) while others said the Almighty would be found outside the movements of history (transcendence of God). Some
beckoned us to what they thought were sacred spheres of
life, which they distinguished from the secular and profane.
Some bidded us to espouse a pure orthodoxy, while luring
us away from what they saw as contaminations of our faith
from our cultural heritage which was alien to them.

We remain unconvinced by theologians who claim they
have found the right combinations of the "either/or" options
and thus overcome the bifurcations. We know by their fruits
(Matthew 12:33) that they have not exorcised the ghosts of
the past which continue to divide the church into contending
factions. We know because we have been caught in the
crossfires! We now regret that so many among us allowed
ourselves to serve as mercenaries in these debilitating battles
over distortions of the faith which are alien to our experiences. We are finding greater resources to combat the bifurcations among Christians who struggle against oppression.
This includes the Black Church heritage and the Korean tradition of resisting colonizers and tyrants.

Beyond the unreal choices which are posed as conditions
for our acceptability, we have an even more restrictive experience with boxes. We are told to operate through the World

Division for overseas matters, while the National Division was to serve our domestic concerns. But can the divisional boxes work together if ethnic minorities want to explore the impact of overseas developments on domestic minorities? Is it possible, to take another illustration, to institutionalize a jurisdictional or national system of deploying ordained persons which would transcend the sacrosanct episcopal appointment system which is geared to the Annual Conferences? Would interdenominational ventures in local churches and community organizations receive as great a support as a center controlled exclusively by a single denomination? Denominations, their Boards and Divisions, and the Annual Conferences are but a few of the boxes which have entombed some of our deepest aspirations. The church has not approached Isaiah's description of the servant of God: "A bruised reed he will not break, and a dimly burning wick he will not quench; he will faithfully bring forth justice." (Isaiah 42:3)

When we consider the suffocating consequences of these oppressive bifurcations and boxes, we are not surprised that these current forms of Laws induce death. Opposing, if not overthrowing, them is a matter of life and death, as Jesus and Paul taught us and illustrated by their lives.

We are mindful of the enormity of the task and its broader contexts. We have been describing only the religious dimensions of the cultural imperialism and cultural genocide practiced by the emerging central focus for Christian reflection and action, namely, the "American Empire." The racist operations of this Empire are but one facet of the domestic expressions of that omnipresent internal-colonialism which also appears in sexism and classism. The overseas expressions appear in neo-colonialism which supports innumerable oppressive regimes abroad. If the Roman Empire was the central focus for faith and action in Revelation, the American Empire is the current focus for Christians on this fragile island in the universe. If the early Christians found in the Roman Empire a contradiction to God's creation, should it surprise modern Christians that we would call attention to racism of the "American Empire" which does the same?

SALVATION, THE CHURCH AND OUR ACTION

We addressed the third question. Is there anything that can be done, and if so, how? We find our understanding of Salvation and the Church serves us well in reversing the problems we noticed in terms of the *sin* of self-preoccupation, which inflicted *Laws* upon others, and prompted *death*. Salvation is achieved by the Spirit who (1) overcomes the bondage and oppression of the Law with the gift of *freedom*, or *liberation*, (2) reverses death's decay with new *life* and (3) leads us into a Church, the *Body of Christ*, where the sin of self-preoccupation is mitigated. We will use the Resurrection of the Body as a suggestive explanation for the meaning of the Body of Christ.

Just as our understanding of Creation and the Fall has led us to say our concern for racial oppression is Christian, so too our understanding of Salvation enables us to appreciate how our expectations for liberation are equally Christian. In fact, by reflecting on our aspirations through the resources of the Bible and tradition, we may have uncovered a seldom mentioned emphasis of our common heritage concerning Salvation which illuminates other people as well, if not the whole of creation! The Apostle Paul writes concerning the widespread relevance of the themes of bondage and liberation. He says that the

> will of God . . . subjected creation to hope; creation itself will be set free from its bondage to decay and obtain the glorious liberty of the children of God. We know that the whole creation has been groaning in travail together until now . . . In this hope we are saved. (Romans 8:20ff)

In our Wesleyan tradition we have held a place for the work of the Spirit—it was primarily personal, inward and emotional. A crucial event has made it so. John Wesley had a heartwarming experience when he was assured that he was accepted as a child of God. He cited Romans 8:16 as an explanation of his experiences on May 28, 1738, 8:45 p.m. at the Chapel on Aldersgate Street in London, England. The text itself reads, "It is the Spirit itself bearing witness with our spirit that we are children of God." As historic and valid as this experience was, recognition of the issue of oppression and appreciation for liberation helps us see other works of the Spirit in the drama of Salvation. The Spirit liberates! "The Lord is the Spirit, and where the Spirit of the Lord is, there is freedom." (II Corinthians 3:12) This freedom does not only apply to the inward life of individuals.

Witness the book of Judges, and the successive waves of liberation movements for oppressed peoples who, only a generation before that period, had tasted initial successes in the Land of Promise. The Holy Spirit is a conspicuous initiator of freedom movements which dethrone oppressors and restore wholeness. (Othniel, Judges 3:10; Gideon, 6:34; Jephthah, 11:29; Samson, 13:25; etc.) Despite their limited advances ethnic minorities are discovering new forms of oppression in the Land of Promise—including the church. Should it surprise us that ethnics seek liberation, and that they are discovering that the Spirit brings them freedom from their bondage?

Besides the freedom which the Holy Spirit affects, it creates new life which reverses the death which the Law produces. "The written law produces death, but the Spirit gives life." (II Corinthians 3:6) By life, we have in mind the surge of faith, hope and love which the Spirit gives—faith in the work begun by God in Christ; hope in its ultimate triumph; and· therefore an outreach in love to participate with others in facilitating God's intentions.

The best way for us to describe the way God can overcome the sin of self-preoccupation appears in the resurrected body of Christ. The body of Jesus which had succumbed to decay under the ravages of the law and its proponents is raised triumphant by the Spirit over death. (Romans 8:11) If the church is in some distant sense the body of that resurrected Christ (I Corinthians 12:12–31; Ephesians 5:31) we may expect that it too can experience the resurrection of the whole body, including those parts which had been denied their opportunity to fulfill their potentials because they were asked to operate under a Law which was alien to them. These parts may have atrophied and died by failure to operate as they uniquely could. With the resurrection applied to this Body we can speak of recovering their life, restoring their rightful place and insuring their contribution.

Once the diversity of the parts of a single Body begins to develop we can expect in human communities such as the church that the coordination of the parts does not come easily. The domination of one part over another must be overcome before harmony of the parts is achieved. In this sense, the emergence of ethnic theologies of liberation among those suffering neo-colonialism abroad and internal colonialism at home signals a historic breakthrough in theology. Much of the Christianity which has been at the leadership in recent centuries has been preoccupied with reconciliation, the harmony of the parts, be it a reconciliation of humankind or between humankind and its Creator. What we are discovering is that there can be no genuine reconciliation before there is redemption, or liberation from domination of oppressive regimes. Redemption has become a primary concern. This makes persisting and excessive preoccupation with reconciliation (harmony, peace, and understanding) sound like a device to avoid fundamental issues.

More likely than not, a full and rightful place for the emerging members of the Body will only be secured after conflicts which will cover a long period of time. If the white members of the Body who presently dominate its structures simply flee the Body or set up separate structures, then the Body will only experience a new imbalance and decay. Only by means of living together through the painful period of adjustments can we expect to see the fundamental sin of self-preoccupation mitigated. New biblical models for self-identification of ethnic minorities and whites could promote liberation from destructive dominations, and facilitate reconciliation among diverse peoples.

For ethnic minorities we are finding a model for a new self in Moses. He illustrates for us how to relate to those in power. We, like Moses, have been adopted by an alien society, trained in its ways, and glimpsed its benefits. But we have come to see that the very institutions which have benefited us at this point have done violence to our people as well as to our own personhood. We recognize that the "treasures of Egypt" at the same time represent "the fleeting pleasures of sin." (Hebrews 11:19–20) The "sin" which we see is the plundering of people of their promising contributions while securing a place for the pampered Pharaohs who offer at best paternalistic service. The same God who initiated the exodus from the bondage of Egypt is, we believe, beginning with judgment and working for salvation within the Church itself. In that work of judgment and mercy we find ourselves challenging the Pharaohs who dominate ethnic minorities with oppressive Laws and promote death in the name of Jesus. Just as the first ship which brought African slaves to the United States was called "the good ship Jesus," those who bear the name of Jesus continue to promote new forms of slavery to cultural expressions of Christianity which violate the contributions we may have to offer.

For the predominantly white constituency in the United Methodist Church we offer the story of Jacob-changed-into-Israel as a model for a new selfhood. (Genesis 32:22–32) Jacob left his homeland because he had defrauded his brother, Esau. He accumulated great wealth in an alien land. Later, he decided to return to his homeland and sought reconciliation with his brother. But on the evening before his meeting with Esau, he wrestled with one like Esau. During the night-long conflict he incurred an injury. We are led to believe that he was a better person for the fight and the wound. His name was changed from Jacob, "a trickster who moves ahead by tripping up others," to Israel, "struggler with God and prevailing." Although he battled a human assailant who inflicted injury on him, Israel can say he actually came face to face with God. He renamed the scene of his painful experience Peniel or Penuel, "the face of God."

The themes could serve well the whites who are open to a new selfhood. Their accumulated wealth and power rests in large measure upon defrauding their brothers, and sisters. At this point in history, they feel as if they want to come home from a life of gaining wealth in a land which is alien to them. They want reconciliation. But can there be genuine reconciliation without restitution and reparation? That is, can there be a humanizing reconciliation other than the route which Jacob traveled before he became Israel? Will we hear white Christians sing with Roberta Flack the hallowed spiritual, "I told Jesus it would be all right if he changed my name"? And are they willing to incur the injury which may bring them new identity, restore health and release new life in others?

We cannot help but find in Jesus a more adequate meaning of this suffering which heals. The way of the cross released new gifts in others because it involved the loss of riches and power. "For you know the grace of our Lord Jesus Christ that, though he was rich, yet for your sakes he became poor, that you through his poverty might be rich." (II Corinthians 8:9) It was a scandalous perversion of the cross which led us to rest it on the poor and the powerless and demand that they endure graciously their deprivation and defraud. No, the cross in its redemptive sense meant that the powerful and wealthy should suffer losses. The drama of Salvation has it that

> *though he was in the form of God, (the Lord) did not count equality with God a thing to be grasped, but emptied himself, taking the form of a servant, being born in the likeness of humankind. And being found in human form he humbled himself and became obedient unto death, even death on a cross. Therefore God has highly exalted him. (Philippians 2:5b-9a)*

The emptying released new life, a resurrected body came into being. If white Christians can relive that story with faith in this liberating, life-giving God, we might see a resurrected Body of Christ with more of its members finding fulfillment.

The same trust in the liberating, life-giving God could enable them to see in their human assailants the face of God as well. We as ethnic minorities know our entrance into the inner sanctuaries of the Church looks like the new invasion of barbarians which was supposed to have ruined the Roman Empire. We strike the same terror, horrify, scandalize and inflict hurts. As Christians are asked to see the divine Lord in the human Jesus, so too the story of Jacob-changed-into-Israel calls us to see in those who would inflict injuries an avenue of healing, a divine face. We are told by Jesus that the resistance to the way of the cross is satanic. (Mark 8:33)

It has become clear from the rich heritage of our faith that true wholeness, or holiness, of the Body of Christ will only come through a cross. As ethnic minorities die to the self-image of a Moses who participates in the tyrannies which hold his people in bondage, they adopt an image of a Moses who confronts their Pharaohs and promotes movements of liberation for their people. If whites die to the self-image of Jacob and become the true Israel, we may move closer to reconciliation within the Body of Christ. In all likelihood a "wrestling match" of sorts will be required for a change in identity. This is at once biblically sound and theologically responsible, given our experience and reflections.

APPENDIX III

In October, 1978, the Author was installed as the Executive Direc-tor of the Multi-Ethnic Center for Ministry at Drew University. The Address printed here was his Inaugural Address which spells out his understanding at that time of the role of such inter-ethnic needs for the church and theological education. Perhaps it has not changed since there still exists "a church within a church."

STRANGERS AT HOME

by

WILLIAM B. MCCLAIN

INTRODUCTION

There is a Chinese proverb that says: "Only those who have washed their eyes with bitter water can see clearly." The history of ethnic minorities in America is the story of those whose eyes have been washed with bitter water, those who have "come over a way that with tears has been watered," and those who have trod the "Trail of Tears." This experience of ethnic oppression has been shared by Native Americans, Black Americans, Asian Americans and Hispanic Americans as they have been treated as strangers at home.

A new interpretation of history is the beginning of a change in perspective. It is only when history, with new agony and new insight, is pondered—a brooding of the past and present in search of meaning, form and perhaps hope— that a perception of what is possible can be clearly seen. It is this ancient lesson, rediscovered by Black Americans through painful and bitter experience, shared by other minorities, that has led these ethnic minorities to address the basic problem, i.e., the ideological role that racism plays in the culture of the North American Christian community.

AMERICAN RELIGION AND RACISM

For virtually all of its years the Christian Church in North America has been dominated by a concept of God created in the image of the white man. This deity had the attributes of Caucasian idealization. The authority and omnipotence of Euroamerican white men were equated with the authority and omnipotence of God. Anglo-American culture, values, institutions and ideals persisted as the norm. Condescension, paternalism and racism have been the inevitable attitudes toward ethnic minorities.

The religious basis of the ideology of the Christian West and the cause of much of the oppression of ethnic minorities is firmly rooted in white domination in all areas of faith and life. Ethnic oppression, racism, exclusion, nativist bigotry, exploitation, confinement and even massacre is the bitter story of ethnic minorities in this country.

WHAT HAPPENED TO ETHNIC GROUPS: ETHNIC OPPRESSION

After crossing the frozen seas of the Bering Straits during the ice age 20,000 years ago, the first Americans became natives to this soil. Proud peoples that they were, they lived abundantly at home in the whole rich North American continent, until the coming of the white man. They were made strangers at home as their land was taken and their "removal" became the federal policy. Their forced removal westward became what the Cherokees call "The Trail of Tears." The loss of their land was also a loss of something of themselves and their identity. For as Chief Seattle put it: "The shining water that moves in the streams and rivers is not just water but the blood of our ancestors . . . Every shining pine needle, every sandy shore, every mist in the dark woods is holy in the memory of and experience of my people. The sap which courses through the trees carries the memory of the Red man."[1] The heritage of the Native American is the story of long-forgotten and broken treaties, desecration of burial grounds and of the revisitation of violence and tragedy at Wounded Knee in the winter of 1973. It is indeed a "Trail of Tears," but it is also a "Trail of Broken Treaties" and a heritage of centuries of injustice against Native Americans who have been made strangers at home.

The story of Asian Americans and the Pacific Americans is the story of ethnic oppression. The use of the term "Asian" to refer to such a diverse group of ethnic families itself is a clue to the problem. While there are some cultural similarities, common problems and common hopes, what Chinese, Japanese, Koreans and Taiwanese share for certain is color and a history of ethnic oppression, myths and stereotypes in this country. Asian Americans are a number of different families each with its own language, history and culture. But none have been exempt from the insidious tentacles of racism and gross exploitation.

Although the Chinese arrived in America in 1848 in time for the California gold rush, they could only serve as indentured servants to the miners. The Foreign Miner's Tax Law of 1856 preventing the Chinese from panning for gold was the first among many laws passed to discriminate against the so-called "Asian Americans." In 1859, a law was passed excluding Chinese from the public schools in San Francisco. In 1870, the Naturalization Act excluded Chinese from citizenship and forbade Chinese workers who had already come to America from bringing their wives and families into the country. Anti-Chinese race riots occurred in cities between 1871 and 1885 where, often for weeks, mobs of white Americans looted, burned and murdered numerous Chinese without any fear of penalty from law enforcement agencies. Because of racism, Chinese were caricatured and feared as "strangers." The white majority projected its own hate and fears onto the Chinese as the "other." The Churches reflected this same attitude and saw them not only as strangers to be feared, but as "pagans" and "heathens" to be converted. The Methodist Church forgot the words in Chronicles: "We are all strangers before thee, and sojourners, as were all our fathers." (I Chron. 29:15) and maintained segregated annual conferences for the Asians.

The Japanese Americans suffered similar experiences of ethnic oppression. In 1906, the San Francisco school board passed a resolution which segregated all Korean, Chinese and Japanese children in a separate Oriental Public School. In 1942, Executive Order 9066 placed more than one hundred thousand Japanese Americans in concentration camps. Even though most were United States citizens they were treated as strangers at home. The ultimate racist statement about Asians as an ethnic group was the dropping of the atomic bomb on Hiroshima and Nagasaki (with clear evidence known that Japan was prepared to surrender) and the massacres and napalm used in the Vietnam War.

The fastest growing Asian-American family are Korean Americans. There are more than 300,000 Koreans living in the United States today, as opposed to 70,000 in 1970. Although these new Americans are not the victims of exclusionary legislation, they are nevertheless affected by discrimination and racism. More than 60% of the Korean Americans identify with the Christian Church. More than a third of the Korean American population is college educated, a percentage higher than that of United States citizens as a whole. Although 75% of Korean immigrants held professional, technical and managerial jobs in Korea, they are drastically unemployed and underemployed in this country. Professional persons, such as ministers and teachers, are often forced to accept work as janitors and waitresses. Ministers who have unusual competence, gifts, graces and experience and, in some cases, advanced degrees from theological schools in Korea, are denied transfers and recognition of their ordination in this country. Language difficulties are a factor in some cases, but racism is a bigger factor.

The Black American experience has been one of enslavement, discrimination and dehumanization. Since 1619 and their landing at Jamestown, Black Americans have been the victims of racism and ethnic oppression. Enduring slavery for 244 years and legal segregation for another hundred years, they are still victims of an ever more complex racism. Legal battles have been won. Protests and civil rights movements have yielded improved legislation. Yet, the emerging conflict over the redistribution of wealth and power and Black control over the institutions which affect the quality of Black lives continues.

Brought to this country in chains and auctioned off as property, stripped of their names, language, religion, culture and heritage and denied citizenship, Black people began their pilgrimage in America. It has truly been "a way that with tears has been watered." Lynchings and hangings of Black people became a recreational activity for whites.

The eve of holy days seems to have been the day of unholy beginnings. The Ku Klux Klan, organized on Christmas Eve, 1865, immediately after the Civil War, rode in hooded robes at night for many years as they lynched, thrashed, hanged, castrated, murdered and quartered Black Americans like animals. When the organization, but not its mentality, became somewhat quiescent just after the turn of the century, William Joseph Simmons, a Methodist minister in Atlanta, Georgia infused new life into a reorganized Klan on Thanksgiving Eve by building an altar on Stone Mountain in Georgia and placing the American Flag, the Bible and a sword there and setting fire to a wooden cross. The cross, which had become the symbol of freedom and liberation for recently freed Black Christians, and the hope for those who were not, became the source of terror and fear. It was indeed a period Benjamin Brawley called, "The Vale of Tears."

A formidable structure of discriminatory laws grew up in the South creating barriers of racial segregation in almost every area of interracial contact. De facto segregation was the practice of the North as Black Americans experienced the continuing effect of a ubiquitous racism. These laws of segregation were to remain in effect until well into the sixties and the force of them still persists. The story of Black people in America is a bitter story of racial and ethnic oppression.

The Hispanic Americans are a pluralism in themselves. They are multiple groups bound together by a mixed cultural heritage and language. "The indelible marks of Spanish, Indian, and in some cases African cultures have merged through the years to create a culture that is neither Spanish, Indian nor African, but Spanish American."² The first Hispanic Americans were an indigenous people—native to the territories acquired by the United States. Sadly, much of the land of these Hispanics in the Southwest was taken by force, the people murdered or evicted to release the land. The story of Mexican farm workers and the exploitation of their labor and their lives has been well documented by Chavez and other leaders and organizers of farm workers.

There are other Hispanic Americans from Puerto Rico, Americans by annexation as the result of the Spanish-American War, Cubans who fled Castro's regime, and other Hispanic Americans from countries in Central and South America and the Caribbean. Many shades of color are represented among the Hispanic Americans and yet a common experience of ethnic oppression. Whether they are rural or urban, middle class or poor, immigrant or indigenous, sun-baked or not, all have been segregated, exploited and paternalized by white America. Grave inequalities in housing, employment, and education have resulted from exclusion and discrimination. Whether in the city *barrio* or the farms and fields, Hispanics have experienced ethnic oppression as a result of racism and cultural imperialism.

While these ethnic minorities differ in background, culture, language, and history, all have suffered and continue to suffer a debilitating racism in North American culture in which the religion of America has played a significant role— both in terms of what has happened to ethnic minorities and how they have responded.

ETHNIC RESPONSE TO OPPRESSION

The story of ethnic minorities in America is something more than the record of the white man's aggression, racism, discrimination, lynchings, broken agreements, intermittent remorse, prolonged failure, nativist bigotry and repressive acts. It is also a record of survival, adaptation, creativity, faith, hope, and protest both covert and overt in the face of overwhelming obstacles.

Religion, and specifically the Christian Church, has played an important role in that response. For most ethnic groups the ethnic church provided a place of gathering and an environment where they could enjoy fellowship, create their own institutions, preserve their culture, and not have to apologize for being who they are. In some sense this was an external acculturation process to adopt "Westernized ways," but in a more important sense it was response to the ethnic oppression and an active, creative retreat from the daily tensions of repressing their culture and attempting to be accepted by the white majority. It is here that we discover the creative genius of ethnic minority theological reflection and the beauty of religion created on these shores as many influences converge to give us new religious insight. Religion becomes the organizing principle of these ethnic minorities and the visible center of life. The ethnic churches become caring institutions, both out of necessity and in obedience to their Lord. At the same time their mere existence and their appropriation of the meaning of the gospel were a protest of the majority ideology.

Some have said that this led to a contextualism in theology

dictated by the situation. But do we know of any theology that is not? Those who offer a disclaimer and argue that their theology is a universal understanding of the faith for all people are engaging in an arrogant falsification of the nature of theological reflection. But it is also at this point that our theological task can best become a reflection of inclusion and a true pluralism, including the contributions of all ethnic groups. It is this discussion of Red, Yellow, White, Black and Brown that Benjamin Reist has called the "pentangular" discussion of American theology which he has proposed.

PENTANGULAR THEOLOGICAL DISCUSSION

"New occasions teach new duties," James Russell Lowell observed long ago. New history also demands new theological construction. It was this truth that black theology discovered and has led us into new ways of approaching our theological task. It departed from the Euro-American way of theological reflection. It moved us from a theology of orthodoxy to a theology of ortho-praxis. It became clear to black theological thinkers that our ethics had outrun our theologies. What black theology said was that the church could no longer engage in what Paul Tillich called the "denial of justice in the name of holiness."

While it is a legitimate criticism that black theology was primarily preoccupied with the color problem as it related to black and white, in the process it led to some more universal theological truths that can be helpful in forging a theological discussion which goes far beyond. Black theology has helped us recapture the truth that Jesus Christ is transcendent to all tribes, cultures, races and ethnic groups, but demands of none of them that they relinquish their identities. As Gayraud Wilmore has observed in a recent article titled, "The New Context of Black Theology in the United States:" Black theology demonstrates that Jesus Christ can be de-Americanized without losing his essential meaning as the incarnate Son of God who takes away the sin of the world by his cross and resurrection."

ETHNIC THEOLOGICAL PLURALISM

The Church of Wesley, with the largest ethnic minority membership of mainline Protestant Churches in America, has a unique opportunity to provide the forum for ethnic minorities to engage in a broadly inclusive pluralistic theological discussion.

One of the purposes of this Multi-Ethnic Center for Ministry is to initiate, encourage and promote that conversation among ethnic minorities in America, and to make us more aware and able to participate in a world context with our brothers and sisters whose faith has been shaped and nurtured by their own cultural experience in Latin America, Africa, Asia and the Pacific.

While bitter memories, ill-fated efforts and premature partnerships of the past counsel that caution and care must be taken in forging a broadly inclusive, multi-ethnic theology, it is clear that the time for that conversation is upon us. Such an effort must not sacrifice the unique and distinctive gifts and identities which each group brings from its own historical and cultural background. To do so is to deny the richness of genuine pluralism and to make a mockery of truth and creation. An ethnic pluralism cannot be allowed to substitute symbols for substance and the Cross of Christ for consensus. We must raise some questions for which easy and time-worn answers will not do. We must probe some problems which mundane solutions will not satisfy.

The gifts of each ethnic group and the truth they have discovered must be boldly placed on the altars of the Church to enable God's people to be more faithful to the meaning of the gospel and the judgment and grace of God in a society bedeviled by the demons of hedonism, classism, racism and sexism, and a church obsessed with pop religion and biblicism that threaten to transform the revolutionary ethic of Jesus into an inoffensive prudential morality.

THEOLOGICAL EDUCATION

Theological education must be re-evaluated in the light of the needs of ethnic minorities and the gifts they offer the whole church. This Center must help us eagerly receive those gifts. The Native Americans educate us in poetry of religious expression, joy in creation, reverence for all things, and a passionate attachment. The Hispanic Americans can teach us to celebrate life and not subdue it. They can provide a joy, warmth, and spontaneity that supplies such a contrast to a technological, pragmatic outlook and the formal and often arid worship of the Anglo Church. The Asian-Americans, out of their long, rich and diverse background, can help us to discover the value of a stress on life-oriented qualities such as joy, spontaneity, intuitiveness, respect for the family and the elderly, an amazing ability to synthesize and to bring unity from diversity. Black Americans can help us learn how to bring joy out of sorrow, to celebrate in the midst of pain, to see the sacred and secular as a unity, to affirm life and to know that the blues and spirituals are but different verses of the same song—one sung on Saturday night and the other on Sunday morning.

This Multi-Ethnic Center for Ministry must help the whole Church in its theological task—tap the subterranean streams which flow together at the deepest levels of our common humanity and needs.

"For we are strangers before thee, and sojourners, as all our fathers were; our days on the earth are like a shadow, and there is none abiding. . . ." But, "Thine, O Lord, is the greatness, and the power, and the glory, and the victory, and the majesty; for all that is in the heavens and in the earth is thine; thine is the kingdom, O Lord, and thou art exalted as head above all."

(I Chronicles 29: 15, 11)

APPENDIX IV

AUTHOR'S NOTE: *This address was delivered by the Author in Chicago, Illinois at a Conference on Black United Methodists and Evangelism, sponsored by Chicago Chapter of Black Methodists for Church Renewal in 1976. While it repeats some of the material already offered, there are some nuances here that are specifically directed toward the laity. The charge from the director at that time, the Rev. William T. Carter was, "You've got to show that there is a doctrine of the Holy Spirit in black theology and you've got to preach it!" I tried. The readers can determine whether you can read with any appreciation what I prepared to preach, given the mandate. It is included here because some of the people who were there wanted to see it in print. Every preacher knows that that is dangerous. Let the reader decide.*

EVANGELISM AND THE HOLY SPIRIT

by

WILLIAM B. McCLAIN

I. WHO IS THE CHURCH?

We as the Christian Church are those who have received the Holy Spirit and are committed to Jesus Christ to continue his ministry of love, freedom, and liberation. We are a minority with a Master, a message and a mission. We are called to constantly witness to his saving power and thus we have a Master. We are called to unceasingly proclaim his Word and the good news of salvation and thus we have a message. We are called to incessantly show compassion and to identify with those who are bruised and broken by injus-

133

tice and oppression and thus we have a mission. The Church which does not proclaim by word and deed the good news that Jesus Christ is Redeemer and Liberator is no church at all. A Church that does not have enough love to care about extending that life to others condemns itself as lacking the *koinonia*, the true spiritual church, within its gates. Whatever else may be admirable about its qualities, it is not the Church of Jesus Christ.

The people of God must not be locked in its stained glass fortress with its multicolored windows, red cushioned seats, crimson carpets, temperature-controlled auditorium and Skinner pipe organ where, as Kierkegaard described, "an anemic preacher preaches an anemic gospel about an anemic Christ to an anemic congregation."[1] The church, in order to be the Church, must be the disciples of Jesus who are engaged in touching the lives of others in order to lift. The Church gathers to scatter. The Church building provides a place for the people of God to renew faith, to celebrate the liberating action of God in history and in their lives and to depart to continue the ministry which Jesus began. To be a Christian is to be a disciple. To be a Christian is to stand with Jesus and to participate in his ministry of love, freedom and liberation.

There has been much discussion in the church recently about the separation of social action and evangelism. The evangelicals have contended that the church must abandon its programs of social action and its fight for social justice and try to "win others to Christ." The more activist brothers and sisters have argued that programs are most important. Neither seems to have grasped the true nature of the church and its mission in the world. Social action and efforts of liberation are not one of several offerings in the cafeteria of churchmanship. Both are equally part of God's salvation. The gospel is both personal and social at the same time. Jesus came not only to liberate us from sin. He came to liberate us from the consequences of sin. The consequences of sin are evident in sinful structures that dehumanize, oppress, exploit, destroy and enslave. The Gospel requires us to confess him as Savior and that confession impels us to identify with those who are bruised and broken by injustice and oppression and to join with them in efforts of freedom and liberation. If we would be evangelists we must also be agitators where economic conditions exploit and political realities deprive people of their God-given right to be free and whole people.

The Black Church in its finest hours of history has not separated evangelism and social action. It has seen them as opposite sides of the same coin. It was true of the "invisible institution" of pre-Civil War days when Nat Turner and Denmark Vesey engaged in anti-slavery efforts and at the same time reached out to their slave brothers and sisters and urged them to embrace the Lord and see his salvation. It was recaptured to some extent during the civil rights era of the 50's and 60's under the leadership of Martin Luther King and others as the Black Church experienced a spiritual revival while it engaged in an action program for change. Prior to going to the street to face fire hoses, dogs and mean white policemen, black folks had been on their knees calling on Him they call God and Savior to be their Protector and Defender. And they walked on by faith. "By faith they went forth . . ." They were in the streets because they had been on their knees. They were confronting a system of wrong because they had heard the liberating Gospel of Jesus Christ proclaimed. They were taking risks and willing to walk into the yawning jaws of death because they had met a man named Jesus who had been 'buked and scorned and had been taken to prison and to judgment. This period brought many into a relationship with Jesus Christ and their brothers and sisters. Many of those came as unlikely candidates. No, the Black Church in its finest hours of history knows no separation between evangelism and social action. To divorce the two is to separate breathing from life.

The Church must be the people of God proclaiming the liberating gospel of Jesus Christ by word and deed. Its existence is inseparable from worldly involvement. The Church not only proclaims the good news that Christ is Liberator and Lord and therefore we are free, it must actively share in the liberation struggle.

II. WHY DO WE EVANGELIZE?

The Church is that community that has received the Holy Spirit and is now ready to live out the gospel. Because we have experienced what it means to humanity to receive the liberating promises of God, we cannot merely accept the world as it is. We have received the liberating promises of God and experienced the outpouring of the Holy Spirit; therefore, we must share it with others. We have received the commission from Jesus Christ: "Go ye therefore and make disciples of all nations, baptizing them in the name of the Father and the Son and of the Holy Spirit, teaching them to observe all that I have commanded you; and lo, I am with you always even unto the end of the world." (Matt. 28:19–20). This is a commandment to preach the gospel, to witness that the power of God is salvation. We cannot receive the good news of the gospel and not share it. We must tell the whole world. I hear an old black woman say, "I just couldn't keep it to myself." Somebody said, "I'll tell it wherever I go."

The day of Pentecost recorded in the second chapter of Acts is pivotal to the mission of the church. It was not the speaking in tongues, as fiery as they were. It was not that men and women were gathered together in one accord in one place from every nation under the heaven—as international and impressive as that was. Pentecost reached its climax only after a man stood up to preach. It was not until Peter stood up and preached with the passion of a man who had been in touch with the living Christ did things happen. People began to ask, "What shall we do?" Three thousand souls were added to the Church only after the Word was preached.

The preaching of the Word is central to the Christian

Church. It is at the heart of Christianity. Not rapping, not unintelligible gibberish, not "sound and fury signifying nothing," not hip anecdotes from contemporary magazines, but preaching in which the Word of God is declared with clarion sound and impassioned hearts that have been set on fire by inspiration and experience of a God who calls us to declare his Word. There can be no substitutes for the proclamation of the Word of God, the "foolishness of preaching," the "inescapable claim" upon us. Jesus did not neglect the blind and the lame, the deaf and the lepers, the poor and the brokenhearted, the captive and the bruised. His gospel of liberation and freedom was a declaraton of the rule of God breaking in like light upon the forces that hold humans captive.

One cannot be seized by the Holy Spirit and remain in one's old ways, inactive and immobile. To receive the Holy Spirit is to be kindled by the Spirit. It means to glow and to burn, to be set on fire so that you become a source of warmth and movement affecting others. But as the writer put it, "No one can say 'Jesus is Lord' except by the Holy Spirit." (I Cor.12:2)

It is because we have been seized by the Holy Spirit and experienced the divine commission that we must witness to the saving power of the gospel, the reality of the divine liberation, that we must "tell the story" of our experience. It is good news because we have been brought out of darkness into light, from bondage to freedom and we must share it with others.

III. TO WHOM ARE WE SENT?

We are sent to proclaim the good news to all who have not heard. And even those who have heard it "seem hungering and thirsting to hear it like the rest."

But there are some who are being crucified on the crosses of poverty, racism, exploitation and slavery and they need to hear the story of freedom and liberation. They need to hear that Jesus Christ has paid the price for freedom already and they no longer have to live as slaves—slaves to a system, slaves to habit, slaves to life styles that debilitate and destroy, slaves to laws that are unjust, slaves to ghetto existence. A new existence has been bought and paid for; we are now redeemed and set free.

We are sent to proclaim the good news of God's grace and liberation to those who need a savior. To those whose lives are caught in the web of sin, we must proclaim that Jesus Christ frees and those whom he frees are free indeed. To those whose lives and daily existence are tainted and tattered by sin and guilt we must witness that we know a great Savior who offers grace to the most destitute. We know because we have experienced his mercy and forgiveness and joyfully witness in service.

We are sent to those whom Jesus proclaimed as the object of liberation: to the poor he offers good news; to the brokenhearted he offers healing; to the captive he offers liberation; to the blind and blinded he offers sight and insight; to the bruised he offers liberty. To all we must proclaim that this year is the acceptable year of the Lord, that "their time under God is now."

Bishop Joseph A. Johnson of the Christian Methodist Episcopal Church commenting on Jesus' healing of Peter's mother-in-law has observed that "the only way to lift is to touch." And he is right. You cannot lift a person without touching the person. We are called to touch persons whose lives are devoid of purpose and are lived out as if there were no Savior. There is a Savior who can give purpose and meaning to life.

IV. WHAT IS OUR MESSAGE?

Our message is what it always was: "Jesus is Lord." He is Lord of the world and Lord of our lives. He is present in the world and in the lives of the people, helping them to struggle for the maintenance of humanity in a situation of oppression. He is Lord because of what God has done through him. The titles given to Jesus in the New Testament, as Emil Brunner points out, are verbal in nature and character. They all describe an event, a work of God, or what God has done through Jesus in and for mankind. As Brunner put it: "Who and what Jesus is can only be stated at first at any rate by what God does and gives in him."[2]

The term *Christos* may be interpreted as the one in whom and through whom God is to establish his sovereignty. The title "Son of God" is functional and suggests an office and the work of the Liberator. The title "Immanuel" is defined in terms of its functional implications because the title means "God is with us." The title *Kyrios* describes the one who rules the Church. The title "Savior" points to the one who is to bring the healing, salvation and liberation for which mankind yearns. We speak of Jesus in terms of what God has done through him and that is the message, the good news that we proclaim. He is our message.

Our message is a message of liberation. Whatever else we may say about Jesus and what he did, the New Testament is clear that his sole reason for existence was to bind the wounds of the afflicted and to liberate those who are in prison. He identified with the poor. He declared in the synagogue that he came "to preach the gospel to the poor; he has sent me to heal the broken-hearted, to preach deliverance to the captives, and recovery of sight to the blind, to set at liberty them that are bruised . . ." (Luke 4:18). And in his death and resurrection he reveals that God himself is present in every dimension of human liberation. In dying on the cross he reveals that God takes unto himself the totality of human oppression; in his resurrection he reveals that God is not defeated by oppression but transforms it into the possibility of freedom. Defeat gives way to victory. Death becomes the means of life. This means that our message to those who live in an oppressive society is that they do not have to live as if death is ultimate. They are liberated from the fear of death and the fear of those who can destroy the body. "Christ has set us free from the worries of social ostracism, economic insecurity, or political death," as James Cone puts it. This is a message of liberation. To live as if death has the last word is to live in slavery. To live knowing that death has been conquered and therefore is nothing to fear any longer is to experience liberation.

The message of liberation gives rise to a message of hope. To those who are caught in the webs of poverty, whose lives are threatened daily by the insidious tentacles of white power and oppression, whose very existence is marked by the struggle to survive, there is hope. That hope arises out of accepting the liberating promises of God. God is present in Jesus enabling the poor and the oppressed to live in the present free from fear of death while he joins them in establishing a future that is different from the present.

There is present in black history and black religion an indomitable faith in the future. In their encounter with Jesus Christ black slaves received a new vision in which a new knowledge of their own personhood enabled them to fight for the creation of a new world. It enabled them to sing "There is a bright side, somewhere; don't you rest until you find it." This faith in the future, growing out of their liberating encounter with Jesus Christ, energized their hope and prevented that hope from being simply an idle waiting. It enabled an oppressed people to live as if that vision of the future is already realized in the present. This vision of the future held a people together mentally as they struggled physically to make real the future in their present. Our message must recapture that vision of hope. For people cannot live without hope. Without hope people perish.

Our message must be that Jesus Christ is the Crucified One who identifies with rat-bitten children in roach-infested tenaments and dope addict fathers whose arms are scarred from the use of dull needles in nasty stinking alleys. He identifies with struggling sharecroppers in the hot dusty fields of the South. He identifies with youths whose dreams have been murdered by inadequate school systems and racist and bigoted teachers. He identifies with the unemployed whose lives are spent in hopelessness and despair. He identifies with the frolicking and delusioned young adults who experience joy with contradiction. To the confused he gives His peace; to the hate-filled He gives His love; to those with torn lives He gives His purpose; to the sorrowful He gives His peace; to the despairing, He give His hope. He is the One crucified on Calvary and yet the Living Christ who is available to the world as the Savior. We do not offer creeds, for creeds differ from time to time and age to age. We do not present the church, for it is the imperfect manifestation of the Kingdom on earth. We do not offer ourselves, for we are sinful creatures saved only by His grace. What we offer is Jesus Christ, the Perfect One, the Redeemer and Savior, the Liberator, the Lord of history, and the Crucified One.

APPENDIX V

This address was given at the Board of Global Ministries Annual Meeting in Atlantic City, New Jersey in May, 1974. The context will be apparent in the reading: a conflict between the evangelicals and the social activists. It is reprinted here without undue editing, other than to remove as far as possible the non-inclusive language which was the accepted parlance of the day, but which is in no way acceptable or preferable to me now. At the time the Address was given, I was the pastor of Union United Methodist Church, Boston, Massachusetts.

SALVATION IS ACTION

by

WILLIAM B. MCCLAIN

I. INTRODUCTION

I do not come to offer rebuttal or advocacy to the claims and positions of the evangelicals nor those of the so-called "lopsided" new mission theology proponents. Rather, I come as a black United Methodist pastor, deeply concerned about the mission of the church to the world, and the application of the liberating Gospel of Jesus Christ.

I want to begin with the proposition that 350 years of black church experience in the Christian ministry has some relevance to the conversations in which this Board is engaged. I believe that the Black religious experience is, as Warner Traynham puts it in his new book, *Christian Faith in Black and White: A Primer in Theology from the Black Perspective,* "revelatory." The revelatory function of this experience is that it

143

throws particular light upon how God has acted in the past
and is acting today among a group of Americans of African
descent who have been the objects of a peculiar kind of
oppression for more than three centuries.

The black religious experience in America is unquestion-
ably predisposed to the beliefs and practices associated with
the Judaeo-Christian tradition. But the Christianity that developed and which continues to develop is a different version of the religion professed by the slave masters and their
descendants. Quite clearly, when the Christian faith flowed
through the contours of the souls of black folks, a new interpretation, a new form, a new style and a new perspective
emerged. Black people responded to the Christian faith in
black folks' own way and not the way of their oppressors. It
is this perspective which I wish to offer to this present conversation. I suspect at least some of what informs this perspective would be shared by others of the Third World, and
the other United Methodists of color.

In a sense we can say that white racism created the black
church and its style of life and perspective. But, perhaps in a
more profound sense, God has created it for a witness to
liberation and reconciliation to all peoples.

II. THE BLACK CHURCH AND FAITH

In some fashion or another, the transplanted Africans to
the American shores as slaves always saw some relationship
between the God whom they met in the African forest,
whose sigh was heard in the African wind, and the God of
Abraham and Isaac, Jacob and Jesus whom the white people
talked about in America. And even when the whites said one
thing about their God, the Africans heard another. When
those who preached said that God demanded the African to
be a slave, the African in America heard the clear call of God
through his prophet: "Let justice roll down like water," and
therefore sang, "Before I'll be a slave, I'll be buried in my
grave."

The life and practice of the so-called "saved" who named the name of Jesus has always been a stumbling block for black people; it has created a crisis of faith. We are constantly aware that it was the so-called "saved", those who named the name of the Savior and the Emancipator who created slavery, brought black people over on a slave ship called "Jesus", engaged in brutal wars and atrocities, dehumanized women and continue now a system of segregation, discrimination and economic exploitation around the world. Black Christians continue to say "but look at what the *saved* have done after they 'named His Name'!" And yet black people have continued to be faithful.

With the possible exception of Communist China and the Iron Curtain churches, no people have known the crises of faith that black people in America have known. It is a critical moment when people who have known the suffering and the pain of brutality and death at the hands of the merciless white men who claimed Jesus as their Savior and Lord could still name the name of Jesus and shout about what that Jesus has done for them. It is a crisis of faith when black folks are urged to give world service dollars and even contribute to building churches to which they cannot go and be comfortable and their sons and daughters cannot pastor. But more times than I can count I have seen poor old black ladies in Alabama untie knotted handkerchiefs to give their world service offering on the fourth Sunday—*undesignated!*

Black folks have been faithful to their understanding of the Gospel. In the face of gross corporate and individual sin of the white church and churchmen, black folks have named his name—Jesus! It has been more difficult for these people but they have been faithful.

III. A GOSPEL OF LIBERATION

Part of the reason for this faithfulness has been the nature of black theology and an understanding of the gospel of liberation. The total ministry of the black church in America has been shaped by what some would call the "secular function of the gospel" in terms of a ministry to the downtrodden and alienated persons. The black church knows nothing of a separation between evangelism and social action.

The civil rights era of the 50's and 60's is one case in point among many. The Civil Rights Movement led by Martin Luther King and others, was as much a spiritual revival in the black church as it was an action program for change. NBC, CBS and ABC only showed the marches, firehoses, dogs and police. But prior to going to the streets, black folks had been on their knees calling on Him they call God and Savior to be their Protector and Defender. And they walked on by faith. "By faith they went forth," sometimes now knowing where it would lead them. They were in the streets because they had been on their knees. They gathered to scatter; they congregated to disperse. They were confronting a system of wrong because they had heard the liberating Gospel of Jesus Christ proclaimed. They were taking risks and willing to walk into the yawning jaws of death because they had met a man named Jesus who had been 'buked and scorned and had been taken to prison and to judgment and crucified. But he had truly taken the inevitability out of history. They were willing to go to the marble halls of government and declare the unendurability of suffering. They were willing to face Capitol Hill because they knew of a hill higher than Capitol Hill—the name of that hill is Calvary.

This period brought many into a relationship with Jesus Christ and their brothers and sisters. Many of those came as unlikely candidates. No, the black church knows no separation between evangelism and social action. They are opposite sides of the same coin; they are impartible pieces of the same reality. To divorce evangelism from social action is to divorce breathing from life. Each is a partial gospel; neither is the whole.

It is not at all strange to black United Methodists that the single most important and prolific source of persons to enter the Christian ministry in the United Methodist Church in the last few years has been from the Black Community Developers Program of the National Division of the Board of Global Ministries. That is supposedly a social action program *par excellence*. Who would dare ask if they are not persons in missions? Who would consider that they are not missionaries of the church?

The black Church does not *program* social action as one of the many or several offerings in the cafeteria of churchmanship. That kind of rationalized, segmental social action programming is foreign to most, if not all, black churches. Every Sunday is Race Relations Sunday. Every organization and commission and board and work area is concerned about the issues of freedom, justice and equality. Every sermon has implicit or explicit social justice references. Calling a person to Jesus Christ is to call that person to survival in the community in this world and to collective work and responsibility in that community. The Gospel is liberation. Liberation is both spiritual and physical, corporate and personal. Both are equally part of God's salvation. And this is the black church's understanding of what Jesus meant when he announced his mission: "the spirit of the Lord is upon me because he has anointed me; he has sent me to announce good news to the poor, to proclaim release for prisoners and recovery of sight for the blind; to let the broken victims go free, to proclaim the year of the Lord's favor." (Luke 4:18–19) Evangelism in these terms is seen as agitation. It does not attempt to by-pass economic and political realities. Nor does it expect to side step the tough issues.

Salvation has a somewhat different meaning from this perspective. The message of the two great awakenings of the early and latter part of the eighteenth and early part of the 19th century was to be saved from hell, fire and damnation. Perhaps this is the difference between guilt and shame. But while the black church knew something of this and the influence of this revivalism, hell fire and damnation was never as real to blacks as to their slave masters. The real message of salvation in black evangelism has been salvation from capitulation, salvation from resignation and despair—from giving up and being crushed by life and the evil forces of the white world. It is salvation in terms of the power to survive—the freedom to survive. The calling is into a new relationship with others who are trapped in the same predicament but who are "safe and secure from all alarms, leaning on the everlasting arms" in a collective fellowship of determination to survive and be whole. And it is always *"We* shall overcome"—not *I* but *we*. The liberation of the oppressed and the fulfillment of life are integral elements of God's purpose of salvation.

Salvation from the black church perspective is a community experience. It is, as Warner Traynham points out, the deliverance of a people, "the salvation of a community." It is only secondarily personal or individual. In this sense, the black church draws heavily upon the Old Testament as a corrective to the Marcian tendency to set the personal aspect of the faith in opposition to the social, to over-spiritualize the historical. Jesus came not only to liberate us from sin. He came to liberate us from the consequences of sin. The consequences of sin are evident in sinful structures that dehumanize, oppress, exploit, destroy. Jesus Christ sought our global liberation. It is the church's task, from the black perspective, to continue that ministry of freedom, love and liberation: to seek bread with dignity, peace with justice, power with love and a whole gospel for a whole world. This understanding of salvation requires us to confess him as Savior at home, which is easier than to proclaim Him as Lord in the midst of many cultures, ethnic groups and life styles. But in whatever culture and whatever place, the true evangelists, the true proclaimers of salvation will always be on the side of the oppressed and the deprived. If not, they are not on God's side. And the salvation preached is something far less than that offered by a liberating Christ.

Jesus Christ is the Liberator of persons from systems that destroy and dehumanize at home and abroad; and therefore his witnesses must be agitators where economic conditions exploit and political realities deprive people of their God-given right to be free and whole persons. To accept such a peace with the world is to create conflict with the Lord. But that Lord is also the Bishop of our souls who gives us an appointment with uncontradictory joy to shout on Saturday night *and* on Sunday morning.

It is this Jesus that I've heard so many older black brothers and sisters ask to be for them "a bridge over troubled waters"—long before Simon and Garfunkel ever knew that there are rivers that seem uncrossable and waters that you cannot go through. It is about this Jesus that I used to hear my Aunt Minnie sing: "O, fix me, Jesus; Fix me for my dying day." It is this Jesus who is as real in the stinking alleys of Harlem and Roxbury and on the share-croppers farms in Mississippi as in the isolated and apartheid-created huts in South Africa.

It is this Jesus who calls us to do his bidding in places where people have no vision and no hope. For

> He breaks the power of cancelled sin,
> He sets the prisoner free;
> His blood can make the foulest clean;
> His blood availed for me.
>
> (Charles Wesley)

It is this Jesus who is a balm in Gilead to the tortuous convulsions of the human spirit. In the midst of depleted lives he is an inexhaustible storehouse of spiritual power and resources. It is his name that calms our fears and sets our spirits free to praise him, while we work unceasingly to change systems and redeem those parts of God's creation which have gone awry.

BIBLIOGRAPHY

Books

Allen, Richard. *The Life Experiences and Gospel Labors of the Rt. Reverend Richard Allen.* 2nd ed. Nashville: Abingdon Press, 1960.

Anderson, William K., editor. *Methodism.* Nashville: The Methodist Publishing House, 1947.

Andrews, E. A. *Slavery and the Domestic Slave Trade in the United States.* Boston: 1836.

Bangs, Nathan. A History of the Methodist Episcopal Church. 2 volumes. New York: 1838.

Barclay, W. C. *History of Methodist Missions.* Volume 1. New York: Board of Missions and Church Extension of the Methodist Church, 1923.

The Book of Discipline of the United Methodist Church. Nashville: The United Methodist Publishing House, 1976.

The Book of Hymns. Nashville: The Methodist Publishing House, 1964.

Brawley, James P. *Two Centuries of Methodist Concern: Bondage, Freedom and Education of Black People.* New York: Vantage Press, 1974.

Bucke, Emory Steven, editor. *The History of American Methodism.* 3 volumes. Nashville: Abingdon Press, 1964.

Caldwell, Gilbert H. "Black Folk in White Churches." In *The Black Experience in Religion.* Edited by C. Eric Lincoln. Garden City, New York: Anchor Books, 1974.

———. *Can Blacks Be Christians?* Nashville: Graded Press, 1973.

Cameron, Richard M. *Methodism and Society in Historical Perspective.* Nashville: Abingdon Press, 1961.

———. *The Rise of Methodism: The Methodist Societies.* New York: Philosophical Library, 1954.

Chreitzberg, A. M. *Early Methodism in the Carolinas.* Nashville: The Methodist Book Concern, 1897.

Clair, M. W. Jr., "Methodism and the Negro." In *Methodism.* 2nd edition. Edited by William K. Anderson. Nashville: The Methodist Publishing House, 1947.

Classified Digest of the Records of the Society for the Propagation of the Gospel in Foreign Parts. London: 1893.

Cleveland, J. Jefferson, ed. *Songs of ·Zion.* Nashville: Abingdon Press, 1981.

Culver, Dwight. *Negro Segregation in the Methodist Church,* New Haven, Connecticut: Yale University Press, 1953.

DuBois, W.E.B. *Souls of Black Folk in Three Negro Classics.* New York: Avon Books, 1965.

Edwards, Maldwyn. *John Wesley and the Eighteenth Century: A Study of His Social and Political Influence.* New York: Abingdon Press, 1933.

———. *The Experience and Travels of Mr. Freeborn Garretson.* Philadelphia: Perry Hall, 1971.

Frazier, E. Franklin. *The Negro Church in America.* New York: Shocken Books, 1974.

———. *The Negro in the United States.* New York: Macmillan Co., 1949.

Graham, John H. *Black United Methodist.* New York: Vantage Press, 1979.

God Struck Me Dead. Philadelphia: The Pilgrim Press, 1969.

Haley, Alex. *Roots.* Garden City, New York: Doubleday, 1976.

Hooker, R. "Athanasius Arrayed Against the World." *Of The Laws of Eccelesiastical Polity.*

Hyde, A. B. *The Story of Methodism.* New York: M. W. Hazen Company, 1887.

Journal of the Jurisdictional Conference of the Methodist Church. The Methodist Church, 1944.

King, Willis J. "The Central Jurisdiction." In *The History of Methodism.* Edited by Emory Stevens Bucke, volume 1. Nashville: Abingdon Press, 1964.

Lee, Leroy M. *The Life and Times of the Rev. Jesse Lee.* Louisville, Kentucky: John Early for the Methodist Episcopal Church, South, 1848.

Licorish, Joshua E. *Harry Hoosier: African Pioneer Preacher.* Philadelphia: Afro-Methodist Associates, 1967.

McClain, William B. *Travelling Light: Christian Perspectives on Pilgrimage and Pluralism.* New York: Friendship Press, 1981.

Matthews, Donald G. *Slavery and Methodism: A Chapter in American*

Morality, 1780–1845. Princeton, New Jersey: Princeton University Press, 1965.

Mitchell, Joseph. *The Missionary Pioneer, John Stewart Man of Color*. New York: J. Emory and B. Waugh, 1827.

Moore, John W. *The Long Road to Methodist Union*. Nashville: Abingdon Press, 1974.

Norwood, Frederick A. *The Story of American Methodism*. Nashville: Abingdon Press, 1974.

Paris, Peter J. "The Moral and Political Significance of the Black Church in America." *In Belief and Ethics: Essays in Honor of Alvin Pitcher*. Chicago: Center for the Scientific Study of Religion, 1977.

Phipps, William. "John Wesley on Slavery." *Quarterly Review*, Volume I, No. 2, (Summer 1981).

Raboteau, Albert J. *Slave Religion*. New York: Oxford University Press, 1980.

Richardson, Harry V. *Dark Salvation*. Garden City, New York: Anchor Press, 1976.

Shaw, J.B.F. *The Negro in the History of Methodism*. Nashville: Parthenon Press, 1954.

Shockley, Grant, et al. *Black Pastors and Churches in United Methodism*. Atlanta: Center for Research in Social Change, Emory University, 1976.

Smith, Warren Thomas. *Harry Hoosier: Circuit Rider*. Nashville: The Upper Room, The United Methodist Church, 1981.

Stevens, Abel. *History of the Methodist Church*. volume 1. New York: Carlton and Porter, 1866.

Sweet, W. W. *Methodism in American History*. New York: Methodist Book Concern, 1933.

Thompson, John. *The Life of John Thompson, A Fugitive Slave*. Worcester, Massachusetts: 1856.

Walls, William A. *The African Methodist Episcopal Zion Church: Reality of the Black Church*. Charlotte, N.C.: A.M.E. Zion Publishing House, 1974.

Washington, Booker T. *The Story of the Negro in America*. 1909.

Watkins, W. T. *Out of Aldersgate*. Nashville: Department of Education of the Board of Missions of the Methodist Episcopal Church, South, 1937.

Wesley, Charles H. *Richard Allen Apostle of Freedom*. Washington: Associated Publishers, 1935.

Wesley, John. *General Rules*

————. *The Journal of the Rev. John Wesley, M.A.;* volume 1. Edited by Nehemiah Curnock. London: Epworth Press, 1938.

————. *The Letters of the Rev. John Wesley, M.A.* Edited by John Telford. London: The Epworth Press, 1931.

————. *The Works of the Rev. John Wesley, M.A.;* volume IV. New York: Emory and B. Waugh, 1831.

————. *The Works of the Rev. John Wesley, M.A.;* volume 1. Edited by Joseph Emory. New York: Lane and Scott.

————. "Thoughts Upon Slavery." In *The Anti-Slavery Struggle and Triumph in the Methodist Episcopal Church.* Edited by Lucius C. Matlock. New York: Phillip and Hunt, 1881.

Wightman, William M. *William Capers, Including An Autobiography.* Nashville: Southern Methodist Publishing House, 1858.

Wilmore, Gayraud. *Black Religion and Black Radicalism.* Garden City, New York: Anchor Press, 1973.

Periodicals and Newspapers

Brawley, James P. "The Methodist Church from 1939," *Central Christian Advocate,* October 15, 1967.

The Daily Christian Advocate. The Methodist Episcopal Church, May 7, 1920.

Time Magazine. June 16, 1980.

Monographs and Articles

"The Black Paper" in *Findings of Black Methodists for Church Renewal of the United Methodist Church,* 1968.

Coleman, John W. "Heroic Black Figures of Early Methodism," 1981. (unpublished manuscript).

Felton, Ralph A. "The Ministry of the Central Jurisdiction of the Methodist Church." Madison, New Jersey: Drew University Theological Seminary, 1965.

Park, Robert E. "The Conflict and Fusion of Cultures with Special Reference to the Negro," *Journal of Negro History,* volume 4, number 2, April, 1919.

INDEX